MW01172430

Portrait of a Radical

The Jesus Movement

DJ Kadagian

with

Richard Rohr, OFM
Allen Dwight Callahan
Huston Smith

Portrait of a Radical

The Jesus Movement

In memory of Huston Smith,

whose insights and passion helped shape this work.

Your spirit lives on in every page,

and your wisdom continues to enlighten us all.

Unless otherwise indicated, Scripture quotations are from the Holy Bible, New International Version®, NIV®. Copyright © 1973, 1978, 1984, 2011 by Biblica, Inc.® Used by permission. All rights reserved worldwide.

All rights reserved. No part of this publication may be reproduced, distributed, or transmitted in any form or by any means, including photocopying, recording, or other electronic or mechanical methods, without the prior written permission of the publisher, except in the case of brief quotations embodied in critical reviews and certain other noncommercial uses permitted by copyright law. For permission requests, write to the publisher, addressed "Attention: Permissions Coordinator," at the email address below.

Project Shift, LLC.

Copyright © 2024 DJ Kadagian.

Portrait of a Radical - The Jesus Movement / DJ Kadagian

ISBN: 979-8-9854846-5-6 (Paperback)

ISBN: 979-8-9854846-8-7 (Hardcover)

Book design by Project Shift

Printed in the United States of America

First printing edition 2022

www.Project-Shift.com

TABLE OF CONTENTS

Introduction

In 2000, I produced my first documentary film series, A Crisis of Faith. This four-part series aired on Hallmark and the Discovery Channel and was featured at over seventy film festivals around the world. One of the primary reasons for its success was undoubtedly the great minds I was fortunate enough to work with, who are the basis of this book.

Portrait of a Radical, the first in the series, showcases the profound insights of three distinguished thinkers. Father Richard Rohr, a Franciscan friar, is renowned for his teachings on spirituality, integrating various religious traditions while emphasizing mysticism, contemplation, and social justice. The late Huston Smith, a celebrated religious studies scholar, was known for his comparative work on the world's major religions and his ability to clarify complex spiritual concepts. Allen Dwight Callahan, a respected biblical scholar and theologian, is acclaimed for his analysis of the New Testament and his exploration of the intersections between religion, culture, and African American history.

I had never produced a film before, but I felt the medium offered the best opportunity to delve deeply into the subject and person of Jesus. My brief stay at Yale Divinity School quickly revealed that I was not suited for a traditional academic approach. Reading, especially due to my dyslexia, was a struggle. It was during this time that I stumbled upon some powerful documentaries produced by a Yale Divinity School graduate, ordained minister, and journalist Bill Moyers. These two series, featuring interviews with Huston Smith and Joseph Campbell, revealed that my ability to learn was greatly enhanced by dialogue, images, and music. I came to realize that if I can learn effectively through this medium, I can take my understanding to the next level by engaging directly with the theologians, scholars, activists, academics, and poets who have inspired me. By meeting them in person, I can ask the questions I need answers to and gain deeper insights from their responses.

It's often said that in the process of making a film, many of the most compelling pieces end up "on the cutting room floor." This is particularly unfortunate when countless hours of powerful, uncut interviews are left unseen. This book reassembles this treasure trove of wisdom and history. By breaking down and carefully organizing the pieces of a vast puzzle, I more clearly see an overarching rhythm which furthers my understanding of the subject. Constructing a coherent linear narrative from those non-linear pieces allows me to recognize and internalize the meaning those patterns coalesce into.

I have laid the book out in ten chapters, echoing the ten "acts" in the film. I provide a short introduction to each, explaining my objective and why I asked the questions I did. This is followed by the actual questions I asked and their responses, which I would later mold into a coherent narrative. As with the film, my objective is to create a "stream of consciousness" with the pieces, as if one "voice" is telling the story in a linear fashion. Each section concludes with my reflections on their answers.

As someone with dyslexia, visuals are vital to my comprehension, shaping my deep connection with documentary films and art. In the film, art plays a pivotal role in driving the narrative, much like in this book. However, the transitions between speakers in the film were not always seamless, making me depend on images and music to provide more fluid transitions. I have strived to replicate that effect in this book through carefully selected artwork. The challenge, though, was finding pieces that truly captured the energy I envisioned for the film.

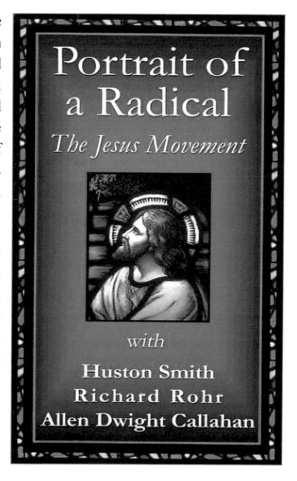

My father lived in Germany for most of my childhood, and for about ten years, I spent several weeks each summer in Europe. We traveled the continent, spending most of our time touring the great churches, monasteries, cathedrals, and museums. This was my only connection to Jesus and Christianity. These were vague concepts to me, particularly growing up in an atheistic family and these encounters shaped what little I understood of the subject. The paintings, sculptures, and iconography, as well as the structures they were housed in, felt heavy, dark, and intimidating to me at that young age. I experienced a wrathful God, a somber Jesus, and frightened people. The gargoyles on the way in and out certainly didn't help.

In the film and now the book, I incorporate artwork that I consider more approachable. Twenty-four years ago, this required spending many nights in the public library, combing through their large collection of art books. Even with all those hours invested, finding more uplifting works that would reflect the theme of the film—unearthing the human element of Jesus and the passionate following he inspired—was a challenge. While the film didn't always call for a lighter energy based on the topic, when I need more inviting imagery, I find frescoes to be a more suitable medium than the dark oil paintings that have dominated over the centuries.

Frescoes often depict scenes of everyday life and ordinary people alongside religious figures.

This blending of the sacred and the mundane makes the scenes feel more relatable and human. They tell stories in a continuous and accessible manner, focusing on narrative and human interaction. I have incorporated them as much as possible where appropriate. My hope is that these images more fully represent the energy Jesus embodies in his time. People pressed up against each other ten deep or forced him onto a boat by the shore so they could all have an opportunity to see and hear his uplifting message. They would not do that with a person they feared or felt intimidated by. I wanted to focus on the energy they were so clearly drawn to.

While I was familiar with the names of the artists when I was creating the film, I was more focused on the process of editing and had not taken the time to learn about who they were—their personal history, motivations, and relationship to their subjects. In effect, how did they come to create the paintings I was working with? This book has several features that I hope will help you interact with the artwork and enrich your reading experience:

- **The Artists** - At the back of the book, you will find a short biography of each of the 45 artists whose 77 masterpieces grace these pages.

- **The Artwork** - Below each work of art, you will find the title and artist, along with a short description of each painting and a bible passage where relevant.

- **The Bibliography** - At the back of the book you will find a detailed art bibliography that includes the website of each painting should you wish to download the images for your personal use.

I believe, in concert, these features will give you the opportunity to put the works in greater perspective and learn more about some of the most influential artists in the Christian tradition over literally thousands of years.

Throughout the book, I have sprinkled in Bible passages that reflect the themes discussed in certain exchanges. I have always been most interested in the "Red Letters," the actual words Jesus is purported to have spoken. These words, found almost exclusively in the Gospels, are denoted in red in the book (or bold in the ebook) just as they are in the New Revised Standard Version Bible (NIV) which was the reference used throughout this book.

You may notice that I gravitate more towards the Gospel of Matthew. It has been said, and I have personally experienced, that Matthew stands out for its structured and organized narrative, making its teachings more direct and accessible. Its focus on Jesus' words, especially through the Sermon on the Mount, offers clear, practical guidance. This emphasis on the Kingdom of Heaven and the fulfillment of prophecy, along with a seamless narrative flow, distinguishes Matthew from Mark's more episodic structure, John's theological depth, and Luke's historical detail. I felt this was most appropriate for the flow of the book.

"Matthew the Apostle," 1612, Peter Paul Rubens. The painting depicts Saint Matthew, one of Jesus' twelve apostles, often portrayed with an angel guiding him as he writes the Gospel. This can be interpreted as a representation of divine inspiration and the spreading of Jesus' teachings.

Keep in mind that the content of this book comes from verbal responses to the questions in my interviews for the film. The style and feel when speaking, is very different from writing. When speaking in an interview, the style is more conversational and informal compared to writing. Answers are usually shorter and simpler to keep the listener engaged and ensure clarity. Immediate feedback allows for real-time adjustments based on the interviewer's reactions. Non-verbal cues like tone, facial expressions, and gestures play a significant role in conveying your message and emotions. In contrast, writing allows for more detailed and structured responses, with precise word choice and the ability to revise for clarity and depth, but lacks the immediacy and non-verbal nuances of spoken communication. I have not altered the text for grammar or punctuation to maintain the same style, tone and flow as captured in the interviews. As a result, the writing may feel different from what you're used to, giving you the sense that you're right there in the room with us. I believe this immersive quality is what makes the book unique and special.

As a final note, I do not claim to be a trained theologian. However, the year I spent producing the film Portrait of a Radical, and now writing this book of the same title, has felt like an immersive education by way of three great theologians and scholars. In a way, I feel as though I have earned my own Master of Divinity through this experience, in a manner that books and lectures alone could never have given me. My understanding of Jesus—how he spent his time on this plane while remaining firmly connected to the divine—has left a lasting impact on me, instilling a conviction that has remained unshaken, even through life's trials and tribulations over the past 25 years.

I hope you enjoy experiencing Portrait of a Radical as much as I did in creating it.

I ..small is the gate and narrow the road

Matthew 7:14

The desert is a place of solitude and extreme conditions, a setting that has historically attracted prophets and spiritual figures from various cultures. The desert is also ground zero for the Jesus Movement. What is it about these desolate landscapes that draws these individuals? In the case of Jesus, is this recounting literal or metaphorical? In the interviews I conducted for this section of the film, my objective is to better understand the reasons behind this phenomenon.

One of the key areas of curiosity is the recurring theme of retreat into the desert or similar isolation. What motivates them to endure such harsh environments? How does the deprivation they experience—whether it be fasting, limited water, or isolation—contribute to their spiritual journey? There is a pattern of seeking out these marginal spaces, away from society's comforts and distractions. What transformative experiences does Jesus hope to undergo in such a setting?

Another intriguing aspect is the rhythm of withdrawal and return. Historical and spiritual traditions often emphasize the importance of stepping away from daily life to consolidate one's energies and priorities. During these periods of retreat, what specific insights do individuals gain, and how do these insights shape their understanding of themselves and their purpose?

Central to this inquiry is the concept of the ego and its dissolution. How does the intense deprivation of the desert experience contribute to breaking down the ego, and what specific aspects of the ego? How does this breakdown of the ego facilitate deeper spiritual growth and transformation, and what stages or phases do individuals typically go through during this process? By understanding these dynamics, what can we learn about the universal principles of spiritual development and the role of hardship in achieving profound personal change?

In exploring these questions, I aim to uncover how Jesus's challenge in the desert exemplifies these concepts and leads to significant personal and spiritual revelations, offering insights into the transformative power of extreme isolation and deprivation.

"Christ in the Wilderness," painted in 1872 by Ivan Kramskoy. This painting depicts Jesus in the wilderness, reflecting on his forty days of fasting and temptation, as described in the Gospels of Matthew (Chapter 4), Mark (Chapter 1), and Luke (Chapter 4), symbolizing spiritual struggle, endurance, and triumph over temptation.

"The Torment of Saint Anthony," painted in 1487-1488 by Michelangelo Buonarroti. This painting portrays the biblical figure of Saint Anthony enduring spiritual torment and temptation, which could be interpreted as a visual representation of the saint's trials and struggles against demonic forces, echoing themes of spiritual warfare and perseverance found in various Christian teachings and traditions.

Allen, how do the geographic and social margins, like the desert in Palestine, play a role in religious traditions and the emergence of spiritual figures?

The desert is simply a place where people don't congregate. It's no man's land. And there is a lot of that in Palestine. The desert is socially as well as geographically on the margins of the society. And we see this in other religious traditions. When we move closer to the divine we find ourselves in those marginal areas out on the periphery of things.

There's a tradition in Israel of prophets coming from the desert or going to the desert or people coming from or going to the desert. This has become routinized. People like Saint Anthony go out into the desert to have this experience, and then they go out and they stay out there and they don't eat anything, and little wild strange things happen to them. They start fighting with demons and so on.

So it stands to reason that some people in Israel would expect that Israel's deliverance would happen in that liminal space. John the Baptizer is one of the famous people who comes out of such a space and lives in such a place. And his liminality can be seen in his diet, the locusts and wild honey and in his mode of dress–the camel's hair coat. You can imagine that it's like wearing a tweed suit with no underwear. And why is this? All of this stuff signifies that he is a marginal figure. He's in that liminal space where God still speaks. Where people can still expect deliverance. John the Baptizer comes out of the desert and he's the person who is, functionally, the advance man for Jesus who also has a desert experience.

"John the Baptist (detail from Altar frontal from Gésera)," created in the 13th Century by an unknown artist. This detail depicts John the Baptist, a significant figure in the New Testament who baptized Jesus, as described in the Gospel of Matthew (Chapter 3),

"Moses with the Tables of the Law," painted between 1624–25 by Guido Reni. This painting depicts Moses holding the tablets of the Ten Commandments, as described in the Bible, specifically in the Book of Exodus (Chapter 20), symbolizing divine revelation and the importance of moral and ethical principles in religious teachings.

In the Israelite context, in the first century, the experience is individual and collective. We know that Moses had his encounter with God in the desert. That Israel received the commandments of God in the desert. That they wandered in the wilderness. That's where their peoplehood was forged. Their national identity was forged in the desert. So the desert has a lot of these associations for good and for ill. One of their traditions is that 23,000 people died at one moment in the desert because of the wrath of God. So it's a liminal place. And in any liminal place, good things happen and not so good things happen. But whatever happens, it's important. It's big.

Huston, how do periods of solitude or reflection contribute to the clarity and focus of individuals, including spiritual leaders, throughout history?

The great historian Toynbee in his ten volume study of history said he found the rhythm going through all history is withdrawal and return. The Buddha went into a thrall for six years, and then he returned after his Illumination under the Bohdi tree and spent the rest of his life treading the bypass and highways of India to teach the Dharma. When the monsoons came that turned the subcontinent into a sea of mud, the monks would come back and be with him, and for three months they would meditate. There is the withdrawal, and then they would go out again. So it's that rhythm of withdrawal to consolidate one's energies, clarify one's priority.

Huston, how do extreme conditions, such as deprivation of basic needs like food, water, or sleep, impact one's perception and understanding of reality, especially in spiritual contexts or practices?

Did he even eat? Did he even drink? In the desert, there's not much water. But there may have been some physiological changes that shuffled in certain ways for his seeing what is really, really ultimate and important more vividly than if he had remained simply in a social context. One can find this also in austerities like fasting, some even go to the lengths of self-flagellation. That seems a little extreme to me, but that's their way.

And then the one that I have experienced most pointedly in my training in a Zen monastery in Japan which is sleep deprivation. Wow, that is heavy. After one night I was permitted to sleep only three and a half hours a night during the peak of this training. Not enough for one for whom eight hours is barely enough. Well, after one night, you're just tired. That's all. After two nights you're bushed, and then you just take it from there. But I can report that if you sustain that, and sleep experiments have proven this. If you keep people awake long enough and don't let them have that sleep, they go psychotic. And I experienced temporary psychosis.

Huston, how do the overwhelming distractions and demands of modern life hinder our ability to introspect and understand ourselves deeply?

We are so harassed by the impingement– no, that's too weak–the avalanche of distractions and demands and duties, many of which we impose on ourselves, that there's no time to know thyself, as Plato had over the academy. Or as the Tao Te Ching puts it, muddy water, let stand, will clear. The mud will go to the bottom, and we can live in a clear ambience. On the most proximate and common sense level, it tells us to be still and know that I am God, whether you want to imagine it out there or in here.

"Lau Tzu," painted in the 18th Century by Ikarashi Shunmei, portrays Lau Tzu the ancient Chinese philosopher and founder of Taoism, whose teachings emphasize harmony with nature and the cultivation of inner virtue. Here he is riding an ox, symbolizing his journey towards enlightenment and the pursuit of wisdom.

The scientists tell us that light bends to the pull of gravity. And we know that a light coming from a cirrus or some distant star, when it passes a huge mass, why, it will bend. And that's the way we look out on the world. We don't see it just as it is. Our perception bends to our ego's demands and insistence that we have things the way we want. Putting ourselves above everybody else in our energies of what we do with our life. We don't take time to be holy, to use another biblical phrase. Aldous Huxley once said that the supreme test of life is to overcome the fundamental human disability of egoism.

Richard, how does shifting focus from concerns about the physical end of the world to the end of personal constructs and illusions contribute to a deeper spiritual understanding? What does this perspective reveal about the process of transformation and letting go?

We've spent so much time worrying about when the world is going to end. I don't think Jesus is concerned at all about the end of the world. He's concerned about the end of worlds. That moment that normally happens to all of us sooner or later, when the world we've fabricated or constructed, our own self-image, our own fame, our own intelligence, our own health, our own youth, our own good looks. When we realize all of that is gone, or it's over, or it doesn't work anymore, or it doesn't mean anything anymore. We're letting everything mirror us, moment by moment by moment. If you never break that addiction to the hall of mirrors, the revolving hall of mirrors of identity and role and persona and prestige and possessions, after 30 years you basically don't have a clue. You really don't. You don't have a clue who you are.

What Jesus is preparing us for is the letting go of these illusions, the letting go of worlds. And that's the language of transformation, which is what a great spiritual teacher is always using. The

"Christ in Gethsemane," painted in 1886 by Heinrich Hofmann. This painting portrays Jesus in the Garden of Gethsemane, as described in the Gospel of Matthew (Chapter 26), depicting his anguish and prayerful submission to the will of God before his arrest and crucifixion, illustrating themes of sacrifice, redemption, and the humanity of Jesus.

11

language of transformation. To prepare you to be transformed into something more. And only those who move into their fears, move beyond their fears, and face their fears, are the ones who can move into something new, into something more. Otherwise, you stay inside of this tiny comfort zone.

I don't think there's much point in worrying about when the world is going to end. But there's a lot of point in being ready to let go of it tomorrow if it's asked of me. That could almost be a total recipe for spiritual growth. Could I so live my life today that if my wife was taken from me tomorrow, my money was taken from me tomorrow, whatever the worst tragedy might be, that I know I could still live? I could still trust God? I could still believe God is good? That's the spiritual question. But that demands the letting go of worlds.

Huston, how does the concept of letting go resonate within various spiritual traditions? What are we letting go of?

What one ultimately lets go of is the ego. This clamorous ego with its demands. Give me this, give me, give me, give me. And it can take many forms. One of them, as one grows older, is time. We want more time. We're like blind men going around with our tin cups. Give me five minutes, give me fifteen minutes, and so on. But, of course, we know that we have to let go of time. That time, as far as our ego goes, is going to come to an end. Socrates said that all life is a preparation for death, and that could be translated to letting go. Because death is the letting go of this world and every ingredient therein.

Richard, why do you think many Western Christians are drawn to Buddhism? What fundamental difference in approach to the concept of the ego and the self distinguishes Buddhism from Western Christianity, and why might some find the Buddhist perspective more resonant in addressing personal transformation?

Many Western Christians, both in Europe and North America, are very attracted to Buddhism. And I've wondered why. As a Franciscan, I was exposed to the mystical tradition, the contemplative tradition. So Buddhism was never a need for me because I was given the same teachings inside of Christianity. But I realized that most Christians–Catholic, and Protestant–were never given that teaching.

Buddhism is absolutely upfront and honest about the problem of the ego. You can't get through Buddhism 101. The first lecture will tell you your ego's in the way. What Western Christianity has done is said that the shadow is the problem, the dark side of the self. Buddhism is real clear about this. It doesn't waste any time attacking the shadow. The rejected self is what I mean by the shadow. The inferior self, the wounded self that thinks it's the problem. It's the center of the world. It thinks it's more important than it is. And by that, we mean the ego.

And what we have is most Christians attacking their shadow, fruitlessly. It only goes underground. It only goes into denial. We keep pretending the shadow is the problem. Jesus never says the

"Shakyamuni Buddha," 18th century, by an unknown artist. "Shakyamuni" means "Sage of the Shakyas." It is a title used to refer to Siddhartha Gautama, the historical Buddha who belonged to the Shakya clan. The title emphasizes his role as a wise and enlightened teacher from this specific lineage.

shadow is the problem. The ego is the problem. So I think Buddhism will continue to be attractive because it names for many people the real problem. I know that Christianity said this too, but a lot of us can't hear it in Christian language anymore. Jesus says, "Unless the grain of wheat dies, it remains just a grain of wheat." He's talking about the death of the private self to enter into the God Self, the Great Self. That sounds exactly like Buddhist teaching. Is it that we can't hear it from Jesus, or that it hasn't been explained to us in a way that we can hear it? He's talking about how do you get transformed? How do you get rid of illusion and the false self to enter into the true self?

"Very truly I tell you, unless a kernel of wheat falls to the ground and dies, it remains only a single seed. But if it dies, it produces many seeds. Anyone who loves their life will lose it, while anyone who hates their life in this world will keep it for eternal life." (Matthew 28:5-10)

Both Jesus and the Buddha conveyed profound insights into the nature of existence and the path to liberation. In their teachings, they emphasized the transformative power of letting go and transcending attachment. Jesus' metaphor of the kernel of wheat falling to the ground and dying echoes the Buddha's teaching on the cause of suffering, which is craving or attachment. Both suggest that clinging to worldly desires and attachments leads to suffering and prevents spiritual growth. Conversely, by relinquishing attachment and craving, one can achieve liberation and eternal life, as Jesus describes, or Nirodha, as the Buddha termed it, the cessation of suffering through the overcoming of craving and attachment. Thus, both teachings converge on the notion that true fulfillment and freedom come from letting go of the ego and worldly attachments.

Samudaya: समुदय

The cause of suffering is craving or attachment

Nirodha: निरोध

Suffering can be ended by overcoming craving and attachment, leading to liberation

Huston, what significance do you see in distinguishing between the human Jesus and the incarnate Christ?

The human Jesus pales in importance with the incarnate Christ and physical facts about the human. Jesus might obscure the disclosure of the implosion of the divine within. This life, and that implosion, which, to spell it out for just a moment, is that the human ego of this life dissolved to make room for the divine in Jesus' consciousness. And it is precisely because that human ego, about which all the historical facts would be related, effaced itself intentionally and deliberately in order that the divine in Jesus might be revealed more completely through it.

Richard, how might Jesus perceive the role of spiritual disciplines, such as solitude and letting go, in addressing the problem of the ego and facilitating spiritual growth?

Jesus knows the ego is the problem. The ego out of control. That's why all spiritual disciplines are about some form of under stimulation. Some form of letting go. All great spirituality is about letting go. That's why all the great spiritual teachers are always sending you into solitude, into the desert, into the belly of the whale, like Jonah, into the place of darkness where you can't fix it. Where you can't control it, where you can't even understand it, and then God spits you up on a new shore. So the prophet is spit up on the new shore knowing something forever that he didn't know, and would not know, had he not been eaten by the whale.

I think Jesus is saying that there's something you know when you've gone through that. Something wonderful always happens because finally you can't sustain yourself anymore, and you have to find out what it is that really sustains you. You meet somebody. I think that's what happened to Jesus. If you remember, the only message he comes out of the desert with, is I'm a beloved son. It's a safe universe.

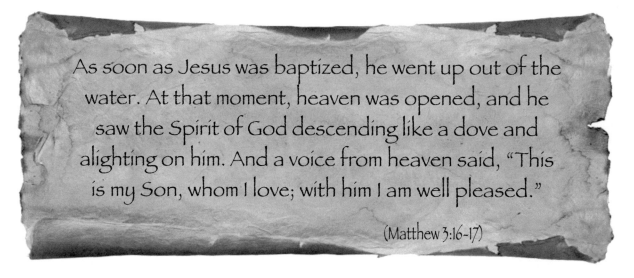

As soon as Jesus was baptized, he went up out of the water. At that moment, heaven was opened, and he saw the Spirit of God descending like a dove and alighting on him. And a voice from heaven said, "This is my Son, whom I love; with him I am well pleased."

(Matthew 3:16-17)

Reflections

The desert is clearly not just a physical wilderness but a symbolic realm where people are removed from the ordinary structures and expectations of society. This aligns with the notion that spiritual growth and divine revelation often require stepping away from the familiar and comfortable and venturing into the unknown and the uncomfortable. The desert as a liminal space serves as a powerful metaphor for the human journey. As Allen observes, liminal spaces are those moments in our lives where we find ourselves in transition, on the threshold of something new, yet not fully out of the old. These moments, though often challenging and uncomfortable, hold significant potential for transformation and growth.

Since my introduction into the world of the spirit, and through the prism of myth and religion, I have been drawn to the notion that profound spiritual experiences and encounters with the divine often occur in marginal spaces. Was Jesus' journey into the desert, as recounted in all four gospels, a literal event or a powerful metaphor? We can only speculate, but I believe it was both. As an avid student of metaphor, I find the idea of a liminal space where big change is possible compelling. So compelling that I wanted to experience that space myself in both of its forms, as metaphor and literal, in the hopes of getting a glimpse of the divine I have always imagined those traveling to a liminal space might encounter.

And so, a number of years ago, I ventured into the most remote desert in the United States and attempted my version of "forty days and forty nights" in search of something more. It was a very difficult time in my life, and I believed that that liminal space would put me in the best position to break through barriers that were clearly holding me back in my own spiritual journey. It was brutally difficult for me—mentally, spiritually, and physically. And all three would conspire to drive me out of the Maze Desert well before my forty days were realized. But not before I got a sense of what could happen inside such a metaphor if you had the intestinal fortitude to stay and the physical ability to survive.

The physical deprivation that Jesus would have felt was real. While we are not in a position to speculate how someone of his nature would experience the desert, we know that the lack of food, water, and shelter from extreme temperatures has profound effects on the mind. We have to expect Jesus, as human and divine, to experience this to some degree. Our modern understanding of fasting and exposure to harsh conditions can help us grasp these effects more clearly.

In the Judean Desert and surrounding areas, Jesus would have experienced swings in temperature between as much as 55-60 degrees—from over 100 degrees during the day to as low as the high 40s at night. These swings would have added to the physical and mental strain Jesus experienced during his time in the desert. The searing heat during the day would have made it difficult to find comfort and conserve energy, while the cold nights would have posed additional challenges in maintaining body heat and ensuring restful sleep. This environmental stress, combined with fasting, would have significantly tested his physical endurance and mental resilience.

Initially, his body would rely on the glycogen stored in his liver and muscles to fuel his every step and thought. But as the days wore on, these stores would be quickly exhausted. In response, a metabolic shift would occur. His body would transition to burning fat for energy, entering a state known as ketosis. This shift, while challenging, had an unexpected benefit. The ketones produced during this process become a potent fuel for the brain, leading to increased mental clarity and focus. The fog of hunger would lift and be replaced by a sharpness of mind that many describe as almost otherworldly.

Physically, Jesus would feel the strain. His muscles ached, and his steps grew slower. Yet, the energy efficiency of ketosis would sustain him, allowing him to endure despite the lack of nourishment. The minimal water he would find from sparse desert sources might have been enough to keep him hydrated. Our physical bodies under these circumstances can be remarkably resilient, a testament to the adaptability of the human body when pushed to its limits. Of course, this would assume he was able to remain at least minimally hydrated.

"The Temptation in the Wilderness," 1898, Briton Rivière. This painting depicts Jesus being tempted by Satan in the wilderness, symbolizing the trials and spiritual challenges he faced, as described in Matthew 4:1-11. This scene illustrates Jesus' steadfast faith and resistance to temptation, serving as a model for Christians to rely on their faith when facing their own trials and temptations.

Spiritually, we know that Jesus experienced a transformation while under these conditions. The initial days would have been the hardest, with his mind wrestling with the absence of food and the stress of the environment. But as his body adapted, so would his mind. The ketones provided a clarity that cut through the noise of physical discomfort. His thoughts became more focused, his meditations and prayers deeper. The desert's silence would likely amplify his mental acuity, turning each moment into an opportunity for profound reflection.

We can speculate that the absence of physical sustenance redirected his focus inward, toward a spiritual sustenance that was far more profound. Fasting, a time-honored spiritual practice, opened a gateway to heightened awareness and closer communion with the divine. Every challenge, every moment of physical weakness, would become a test of his faith. And with each test, perhaps experienced as the three temptations, his spiritual resilience would grow. He likely found strength not in his body, but in his unwavering connection to the divine. The physical deprivation underscored a powerful truth: the spirit could transcend the limitations of the flesh.

In this state, Jesus functioned as an integrated whole—physically enduring, mentally sharp, and spiritually profound. The desert, with all its harshness, became a place of transformation. It was here, in the midst of physical desolation, that Jesus clearly experienced a profound spiritual and mental awakening, preparing him for the trials that lay ahead.

Not for want of trying to experience even a sliver of the divine with Jesus as my example, I would quickly realize that unintended fasting due to illness, coupled with inadequate hydration, can lead to physical and mental fatigue, dizziness, and difficulty concentrating as the body struggles to maintain homeostasis. It did not help that I sustained a major injury during a fall early in my journey that would later require surgery to have a titanium plate inserted in my neck to hold together multiple crushed vertebrae—damage that has resulted in permanent nerve damage and its many attendant complications.

While it was clear I was not physically in a state to withstand any more physical abuse, I cannot say with conviction that I could have endured the mental assault I was experiencing for a full forty days and nights. However, the experience did give me insight into why, as Father Rohr explains, Jonah entered "the belly of the whale" in the first place. It did begin to move the needle for me.

Metaphors aside, in more relatable terms, I was attempting what the Buddhists might term ego dissolution. While different religious traditions and spiritual practices approach the challenge of the ego differently, there is a fundamental unity in their teachings regarding spiritual transformation. Both Eastern traditions like Buddhism and Western religions like Christianity emphasize the need to transcend the ego and discover one's true self. This shared insight underscores the universality of spiritual truths and the human quest for enlightenment.

Buddhism's direct confrontation of the ego offers an intriguing perspective on the differences

"The Temptation of Christ," 1854, Ary Scheffer. This painting depicts Jesus being tempted by Satan in the wilderness, highlighting the moment Satan offers Jesus all the kingdoms of the world if he will bow down and worship him, as described in Luke 4:5-8. This scene underscores Jesus' rejection of earthly power and glory in favor of spiritual integrity and obedience to God, emphasizing the importance of prioritizing spiritual values over worldly temptations.

between Buddhist and Christian approaches to spiritual growth that I explored with Father Rohr. He postulates that while Buddhism openly acknowledges the ego as a central obstacle to enlightenment, Western Christianity often focuses on confronting the shadow or darker aspects of the self. He suggests that this emphasis on the shadow may obscure the fundamental similarity between the two traditions in addressing the ego's role in spiritual transformation.

By highlighting Buddhism's clarity in addressing the ego, Rohr prompts Christians to reexamine their own tradition and teachings. He suggests that if Christians delve deeper into their spiritual heritage, they may find parallels to Buddhist insights, particularly regarding the ego's significance in the journey toward self-transcendence. His perspective encourages Christians to recognize that despite surface differences, both traditions ultimately speak to the need for ego dissolution and the realization of a deeper, more authentic self. The concept of letting go is echoed in Luke 9:23-24.

The desert's duality as a place of both peril and promise mirrors our own experiences of being in the between phases of life, reminding us that moments of isolation and uncertainty can be fertile ground for profound insight and renewal. The narratives of John the Baptist, Jesus, and the Israelites emphasize that these transitions, though difficult, are essential for forging identity and understanding one's purpose in the larger journey of life.

Father Rohr's emphasis on the message Jesus brings out of the desert—the affirmation of being a beloved son in a safe universe—underscores the profound shift in perspective that can result from surrendering to the unknown. This, in turn, marked the beginning of the Jesus Movement. And the world would never be the same.

Then he said to them all: "Whoever wants to be my disciple must deny themselves and take up their cross daily and follow me. For whoever wants to save their life will lose it, but whoever loses their life for me will save it." (Luke 9:23-24)

Three patron saints that journeyed into seclusion and inspired movements

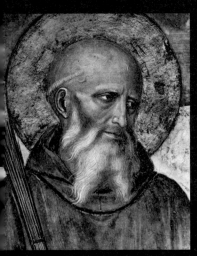

Saint Benedict, a Christian monk from the 6th century, played a pivotal role in shaping Western monasticism. Renowned as the founder of this tradition, his enduring legacy rests upon the Rule of Saint Benedict, a comprehensive framework delineating the principles of monastic existence. This Rule, characterized by its emphasis on prayer, labor, and communal living, served as a beacon guiding countless individuals toward spiritual enlightenment. The Benedictine order, established upon these teachings, emerged as a cornerstone of medieval religious life, fostering a harmonious balance between devotion and duty. Through his profound insights and steadfast dedication, St Benedict left an indelible mark on the trajectory of monasticism in Europe, shaping its course for generations to come.

Despite his lasting influence, Saint Benedict's relationship with organized religion of his time was not without tension. Benedict initially sought solitude as a hermit in Subiaco to escape what he perceived as the moral decay of society, including within the Church. His strict adherence to a life of prayer and asceticism attracted followers, leading to the formation of several monastic communities. However, his rigid standards and uncompromising vision for monastic life were met with resistance. According to tradition, some monks even attempted to poison him, unable to cope with his stringent reforms.

Benedict's Rule itself was a response to the laxity he observed in other monastic communities. It provided a structured yet moderate path that contrasted sharply with the more austere practices of earlier desert monasticism. His vision of a self-sufficient, communal monastic life, dedicated to both work and prayer, offered a practical and spiritually fulfilling alternative that ultimately gained widespread acceptance.

Saint Francis, a revered figure from 13th-century Italy, left an indelible mark on the Christian world as the founder of the Franciscan Order. His unwavering commitment to poverty, humility and universal love epitomized his fervent desire to emulate the life of Christ. Notably, he extended his compassion not only to fellow humans but also to all living beings, earning him renown for his interactions with nature and animals, including his famed sermons to birds. Among his literary contributions is the "Canticle of the Sun," a poignant ode celebrating the beauty and interconnectedness of God's creation. Saint Francis's enduring legacy is encapsulated in the enduring values of the Franciscan tradition: simplicity, solidarity with the marginalized, and reverence for the natural world.

Despite his veneration today, Saint Francis's relationship with the established Church was marked by tension and challenge. Born into a wealthy merchant family, Francis experienced a profound spiritual transformation that led him to renounce his wealth and adopt a life of radical poverty. This radical approach initially alarmed church authorities and his family, as it starkly contrasted with the prevalent clerical opulence and the established social order.

Francis's insistence on living in absolute poverty and his critique of material wealth posed a direct challenge to the Church's structure and the behavior of its clergy. He and his followers, known as the Friars Minor, lived among the poor, preaching repentance and the love of God, which often brought them into conflict with local ecclesiastical authorities. Despite these challenges, his genuine piety and commitment gradually won him acceptance. In 1210, he gained approval from Pope Innocent III to form a new religious order, although this acceptance did not come without scrutiny and the need for Francis to demonstrate his loyalty to the Church's doctrines.

Francis's simplicity and his refusal to own property even as an order, emphasizing mendicancy and trust in divine providence, distinguished the Franciscans from other monastic orders. His approach also influenced the Church to reconsider its relationship with wealth and to be more responsive to the needs of the poor. In addition to his theological impact, Francis's love for creation and his identification with the poor had lasting cultural and spiritual implications. His devotion to Christ's teachings and his love for nature inspired a sense of kinship with all of creation, which is reflected in the Franciscan emphasis on environmental stewardship and social justice. His legacy continued to inspire reform within the Church and among the faithful, calling for a return to the simplicity and humility of the Gospel.

Saint Dominic, a Spanish priest from the 13th century, is a pivotal figure in medieval Christianity. Known for founding the Dominican Order, or the Order of Preachers, Dominic sought to combat heresy and uphold orthodox Christian doctrine. He emphasized education, preaching, and missionary work to promote spiritual enlightenment and safeguard the purity of faith. His dedication to intellectual inquiry fostered rigorous scholarship and theological discourse, strengthening the foundations of scholasticism and expanding the medieval Church.

Despite his profound impact, Saint Dominic's relationship with the broader Church and society was not without tension. His mission to combat heresy, particularly the Albigensian heresy in southern France, placed him at the heart of religious conflicts. The methods employed by the Dominicans, including rigorous preaching and sometimes harsh measures, were controversial and led to friction with local authorities and other ecclesiastical figures.

Dominic believed that education and clear theological teaching were the best tools to achieve his goals. The establishment of the Order of Preachers was rooted in the need for a learned and articulate clergy capable of defending orthodox doctrine. This focus on education and debate laid the groundwork for scholasticism, a method of critical thought that dominated medieval universities and was essential to the Church's intellectual life.

Dominic's efforts were instrumental in forming universities and promoting higher learning within the Church. The Dominicans became renowned for their intellectual rigor and dedication to teaching, significantly influencing theological and philosophical discourse. Figures like Thomas Aquinas, a Dominican friar, emerged as leading scholars whose works remain foundational in Christian theology.

Paintings in order Fra Angelico 1441, Fra Angelico 1442-1445, Cimabue 1278-1280

"Who do the crowds say I am?"

Luke 9:18

Throughout human history, Jesus has remained a figure enshrouded in layers of mystery and misconception. Yet his presence carries an ineffable allure that transcends time and resonates across diverse cultural landscapes. Whether contemplated as the historical "Son of Man" or revered as the spiritual "Son of the Father," his enduring influence over 2,000 years has forever changed human history.

In this segment of the film, my objective is to peel back the layers of theological interpretation and uncover the essence of Jesus as a person. This second chapter touches on his physical attributes, educational background, familial lineage, and the socio-cultural environment of his time. The scarcity of historical records detailing his formative years adds to the mystique surrounding his early life, leaving us all to speculate on what shaped him and drove the movement he would lead.

Additionally, I seek to examine the evidence substantiating his historical existence and shed light on the duration of his ministry. While the New Testament provides accounts of Jesus' teachings and miracles, particularly in the Gospels, corroborating historical references from non-biblical sources are scarce. However, the consensus among scholars affirms Jesus' presence in first-century Palestine and his role as a charismatic preacher and healer. The duration of his ministry, typically estimated to have lasted around three years, is inferred from biblical narratives, particularly the synoptic gospels.

This section of questions and answers, as expected, is brief. However, if there is anything I have learned in the research I undertook in documentary filmmaking, writing, and even quantum economics, it is often in what we do not see that we gain as much insight into our subjects as what we do. In my reflections at the end of each chapter, this is a technique I lean on in an attempt to add more depth of content and context to the story we are able to tell in the film about the person of Jesus.

"The Last Judgment (detail from the Scrovegni Chapel frescoes)," 1306, by Giotto di Bondone. This painting depicts Christ in majesty, surrounded by angels and the resurrected souls being judged, with the blessed ascending to heaven and the damned descending to hell. It relates to the Gospel of Matthew, specifically Matthew 25:31-46.

Allan, what aspects of Jesus' life, particularly his upbringing, education, and early years as a prophet, remain shrouded in mystery?

We don't know a lot about Jesus in biographical terms. If you wanted to write a biography of Jesus, you'd want to know something about his upbringing, where he grew up, where he went to school, what he studied, how he got his journeyman's license to be a prophet, who his friends were, what were the major influences in his life. We know nothing about that. We know a little about his public career, which maybe lasted about three years, give or take. And it's that three-year slice of his life that has had the extraordinary impact on Western civilization and by extension all of history. It's pretty remarkable.

Perhaps among other things, it suggests that the quality of what he did and the effect that it had on people was really what was so memorable and not so much where he went to school or the people with whom he studied or other things that tend to mean so much to us now. I think that everybody who responds to Jesus in one way or another thinks that there's some "thing" that makes him captivating, that explains why he's had such a hold on people. And I think that that one thing, whatever it is, is different for almost everybody.

Huston, what historical evidence do we have regarding Jesus when he first appeared on the scene to begin his ministry?

We know, factually very little about Jesus' life. He wrote a word or two in the sand, which isn't even recorded. There are no physical descriptions of his appearance. As a historian of religion, I

contrast that with Muhammad where we have oceans of physical facts about him and what he said at every stage along the way. It leads one to wonder, how did it happen that a person about whom we know historically so little had that impact? During his actual time on earth, the recorded time is very brief. Three years. Why was the impact so dramatic? What happened to the Earth to have such a shift in consciousness by this one figure? The answer doesn't lie with history as though that's the answer. He took the lead and provided the receptacle at that moment of time for this incursion.

Father Rohr, there seemed to be something so compelling about Jesus that people flocked to him. Not just his teachings but the person himself. How would you account for this?

If we look at the images of Jesus, the pictures even of Jesus, in human history, from different cultures, we see that we were

"Legend of St. Francis: Sermon to the Birds (detail from the Basilica of San Francesco frescoes)," 1297-1299, by Giotto di Bondone. This painting depicts St. Francis of Assisi preaching to a flock of birds, symbolizing his love for all of God's creatures and his belief in the universal ability to understand the divine message.

trying to present him very much as a spiritual teacher. One of the reasons I think I became a Franciscan, a follower of St. Francis, is because what Francis loved was the humanity of Jesus. And that always attracts people. True human beings attract human beings. You can't resist them. You want to be around them. Because there's something so rich and real about them that you want them to rub off on you. I think the reason people follow Jesus so desperately is he exemplified a humanity that was rich and deep and seductive. Most of us aren't that different today.

We don't know his degree of education, but he is not a priest. He's not a Levite. He's not a part of the establishment religious class. He does not do most of his teaching inside synagogue or temple. I think it's very symbolic that Jesus is a layman. Highly mystified people who might be thought of as spiritual actually were more prone to mistrust them. But a human being, a true mensch, as the Jewish people say, you can't resist them. You want to be like them, you want to be close to them.

Opposite page - "The Ascension of Jesus in the Guise of a Priest," from the Dastan-i Masih series, 17th century, artist unknown. It depicts Jesus ascending to heaven, watched by his disciples, signifying his departure from Earth and return to the Father. It relates to the Gospel of Luke 24:50-53, which describes Jesus blessing his disciples before being taken up into heaven.

Huston, there seemed to be something so compelling about Jesus that people flocked to him. Not just to hear his teachings that were to come. But to just be near the person himself. How would you account for this?

We speak of people as charismatic. And I'm sure that you have known people in your own circle. There are certain people who just when they step in the room, why, a new electricity goes on, and people turn to them. I'm talking now just about our every day encounter with that. But, in the case of Jesus, you put a jack under charisma, and you just keep on going.

He would see a fisherman and say "Come on, you've got something more in you than catching fish. I'll make you a fisherman." And they'd drop everything and just cut their ties and go with him. And it carries over into the masses. Crowds so great that he can't press through them, and they will stay three days and three nights.

"The Calling of St. Peter (detail from the fresco the Collegiata di San Gimignano frescoes)," 14th century, by Barna da Siena. It depicts the moment Jesus calls Peter to be his disciple, showing Peter leaving his fishing boat to follow Christ. It relates to the Gospel of Matthew, specifically Matthew 4:18-20, where Jesus calls Peter and his brother Andrew to become "fishers of men."

"Christ Preaching to the Multitudes," 1867, James Smetham. This painting depicts Jesus addressing a large crowd, sharing his teachings and parables about the Kingdom of Heaven with the gathered people as described in Matthew 13:3-9.

One day as Jesus was standing by the Lake of Gennesaret, the people were crowding around him and listening to the word of God. He saw at the water's edge two boats, left there by the fishermen, who were washing their nets. He got into one of the boats, the one belonging to Simon, and asked him to put out a little from shore. Then he sat down and taught the people from the boat.

(Matthew 13:3-9)

I think of Socrates. Socrates has this charisma for his students. They just lived for the time when they could be in his presence. There are different kinds of charisma, and great artists, great politicians have some of that quality, but those are only the foothills, the approximation. Jesus, and Socrates, and the Buddha are the three that stand at the top of my list.

And when you get into that, that different echelon of charisma, there is only one explanation, and that is that they have opened their lives to the incursion of the Spirit. And here, I am using Spirit with a capital S, which is the same as the ultimate reality in the universe. They have opened their lives to the point where they have become simply, I started to say, a container for spirit, but that's wrong. They are conduits for the spirit. So that spirit comes from them. With regard to Jesus, he had become you might say, nothing of himself, if we think of himself as an ego, and simply an empty vessel through which the Spirit channeled through him to spread out to the multitude.

Reflections

It is widely believed among scholars and historians that Jesus lived and grew up in Nazareth, a town in the region of Galilee in ancient Israel. The Gospels consistently refer to Jesus as "Jesus of Nazareth," indicating his association with the town. Additionally, historical and archaeological evidence supports the existence of Nazareth as a settlement during the time of Jesus.

The Gospel accounts describe Jesus' upbringing in Nazareth, where he lived with his family, including his mother Mary and earthly father Joseph, who was a carpenter. The New Testament also mentions Nazareth in various contexts, such as Jesus' rejection by his hometown (Luke 4:16-30) and the disbelief of the people there (Matthew 13:53-58). Modern-day Nazareth is believed to be the same Nazareth associated with Jesus' childhood. While the city has undoubtedly undergone changes and development over the centuries, archaeological evidence and historical records support the continuity of settlement in the area from antiquity to the present day.

There are a small number of references to Jesus as a historical figure in writings by non-Christian authors from the first century and early second century. Two in particular that stand out were written by a Jewish and a Roman historian.

Flavius Josephus, a Jewish historian writing in the first century AD, briefly mentioned Jesus in his work "Antiquities of the Jews." He described Jesus as a wise man, a doer of startling deeds, and a teacher who attracted many followers, both among Jews and Greeks. Elements written by Flavius Josephus generally make his references more credible as he lived between approximately 37 AD and 100 AD. Some argue that his writings may have been altered or added to by later Christian scribes, while others contend that they contain authentic elements from Josephus

"Distant View of Nazareth," 1875, by William Holman Hunt. This painting depicts a distant view of the town of Nazareth, likely from a biblical perspective, capturing the landscape and architecture of the region. Nazareth is significant in Christian tradition as the hometown of Jesus, mentioned in the Gospel of Matthew and other biblical accounts.

himself. The consensus leans towards the view that while the writing likely originated from Josephus, it may have undergone some alterations.

Tacitus, the Roman historian writing in the second century AD, referred to Jesus and early Christians in his work "Annals." His mentions are generally considered authentic by scholars. Tacitus was a respected Roman historian known for his meticulous research and accurate portrayal of historical events. His reference to Jesus and early Christians provides external confirmation of their existence and the persecution they faced under Nero's rule. He mentioned Jesus as the founder of the Christian movement and described how the Roman emperor Nero blamed Christians for the Great Fire of Rome in 64 AD. Tacitus characterized Christianity as a "pernicious superstition" and described the persecution of Christians under Nero's reign. However, whether he had first-hand knowledge of Jesus and his ministry is a matter of debate among scholars.

While there are occasional claims and speculations about ancient inscriptions or documents indirectly reflecting the existence of Jesus or his family, these assertions are highly debated and lack conclusive evidence. The historical evidence for Jesus' existence primarily comes from Christian and non-Christian sources from the first century AD, such as the New Testament, Flavius Josephus, and Tacitus.

There are no mentions of Jesus' appearance. To a Westerner, it is hard to be satisfied with who Jesus was without knowing what he looked like. To fill this gap and perhaps relate to him more closely, we have generally depicted him with European features as opposed to Middle Eastern— the region where he was from. In paintings and icons, we very often see him with light brown hair, fair skin, and in some cases, blue eyes. Coming from the region he did, these depictions may be inaccurate.

Based on historical and cultural context, Jesus' appearance likely reflected his Jewish heritage and the typical features of people living in the region during his time. He would more likely have had a Middle Eastern appearance, with dark hair and eyes, and likely a beard, as was customary for Jewish men of that era. His skin tone might have been olive to darker complexion, influenced by the Mediterranean climate of the region.

"The Transfiguration (detail)," painted in 1518-1520, by Raffaello Sanzio. This detail depicts the moment of Christ's transfiguration on Mount Tabor, described in the Gospel of Matthew (Chapter 17), where Jesus' appearance becomes radiant as he converses with Moses and Elijah, symbolizing the fulfillment of the Law and the Prophets.

Does it even matter what Jesus looked like? Does it have any relevance to his teachings? I would think that would be a resounding no. To my mind, leaving this a complete mystery in the Bible had one positive and one negative outcome. The benefit would be that it gave us license to project our own version of Jesus' physical characteristics onto Jesus. While not all cultures did this, it is understandable that many would so they could more readily relate to him. Looking like one of them would make him more relatable and his message easier to receive. We can clearly see this reflected in images of him from around the world. And in many cases, it is not just the paintings, icons, and sculptures that reflect this cultural bias, but the environment itself in which he is depicted.

The clear downside to this is the friction it created between groups that would later want to claim Jesus as "their own." Imagine a person of western European descent being confronted by an image of a black Jesus. The thought would be inconceivable, to the point of heresy. But there are cultures that have a relationship that dates back much further than our own and were in closer proximity to his region.

One notable example is the Ethiopian connection to Jesus and Christianity. Ethiopia boasts a rich Christian tradition dating back to the early centuries of the faith. According to Ethiopian tradition, the Queen of Sheba, mentioned in the Bible, had a son with King Solomon, leading to the establishment of the Solomonic dynasty in Ethiopia. This lineage is believed to have preserved the Ark of the Covenant, making Ethiopia a significant center of Christian heritage. Ethiopian Christianity has its own distinct rituals, practices, and interpretations of biblical stories, including the life of Jesus. In Ethiopian art, Jesus is often depicted with dark skin, reflecting the ethnic diversity of the region.

"The Last Supper," 18th Century by unknown artist. This Ethiopian painting is a vivid and expressive representation of the Last Supper. It reflects the rich Christian heritage of Ethiopia, which has a long and unique tradition dating back to the 4th century when Christianity became the state religion. Its stylistic features and symbolic depth offer a unique glimpse into the devotional practices and theological expressions of the time.

嶺南陳緣督大寫

Similar tensions arise in other cultures with historical connections to Christianity. For instance, in the Middle East, where Christianity originated, there are diverse ethnic groups such as Arabs, Kurds, and Assyrians, each with their own cultural interpretations of Jesus. Additionally, in regions where Christianity spread through colonialism, indigenous peoples may have adopted Christian beliefs while maintaining their own cultural identities, leading to unique interpretations of Jesus' appearance and message.

Matthew and John traveled with Jesus. They knew what he looked like. Why did they not include any description of Jesus' appearance when there are many references made about his powerful presence? Did later Christians remove descriptions they may have included? In retrospect, the fact that we don't know what Jesus looked like made it more likely that people would be inclined to listen to his message. Was this intentional, by accident, or by divine intervention?

We know very little about Jesus' family. In the Gospels, Jesus rarely spoke of his family and never mentioned any by name. This is not what one would expect when considering the cultural context of first-century Judaism, where family was highly valued and familial ties held significant importance. At the same time, Matthew was one of Jesus' twelve disciples and John was also among his inner circle of disciples, so it would be reasonable to assume that they would have been present at various times when Jesus interacted with his family members.

Finally, we do not know exactly how long Jesus' ministry lasted, and we know nothing about his education. We can say with some confidence that the approximate duration of his ministry was about three years, which can primarily be inferred from the accounts provided in the Gospels. The most direct explanation is the mention of Jesus attending Passover in Jerusalem multiple times during his ministry. Since Passover is an annual event, scholars use these references to estimate the length of Jesus' ministry. For example, John's Gospel records three Passovers occurring during Jesus' ministry (John 2:13, 6:4, 11:55-57), suggesting a span of around three years.

In essence, our understanding of the historical Jesus comprises both concrete elements and speculative aspects. What's notable, as I mentioned, is that sometimes what isn't explicitly stated can be as revealing as what is. In the case of the historical Jesus in particular, this is what we must lean on most heavily. And maybe that's the whole point. As Huston Smith so presciently asks and answers, "How did it happen that a person about whom we know historically so little had that impact? It is that the human Jesus pales in importance with the incarnate Christ and physical facts about the human. The historical Jesus might obscure the disclosure of the implosion of the divine within."

"The Life of Christ," 1938, Unknown Artist, This image of Jesus' baptism offers a glimpse into two distinct cultural and religious traditions, illuminating Christianity's interpretation and depiction within the context of Chinese artistic expression.

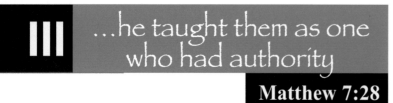

III   ...he taught them as one who had authority

Matthew 7:28

Despite the limitations in our knowledge of the historical Jesus, the Gospels offer a rich window into his teachings, particularly the synoptic Gospels, which capture and largely corroborate the encounters he had and the core message he was communicating.

Three aspects of his manner of speaking intrigue me. First, coming out of "nowhere" and having no training as a rabbi or teacher, how did he establish his authority? How did he so quickly get the ear of the people without any "street-cred," as we might say now?

The second is his use of metaphors and parables to communicate his message. As a student of Joseph Campbell, I deeply appreciate the power of these narrative tools to resonate with diverse audiences simultaneously. This aspect demands further exploration.

Equally important is understanding the manner of his speech itself. What is his tone? Is his delivery forceful or gentle, passionate or restrained? Does his approach vary when addressing different classes and cultures? This interest stems from my childhood experiences in those European cathedrals and museums, where depictions of a wrathful God stood in stark contrast to the bland sermons I often heard in church. Jesus delivered a powerful, provocative, and challenging message, yet much of its impact seemed "lost in translation" in these encounters.

As I delve deeper into the Gospels, I realize that neither impression aligns with the vibrant figure I encounter in the texts. His teachings, and the reactions of his audience in particular, regardless of their background, paint a very different picture. The power of Jesus' message and the way in which he delivered it could not have come across as either intimidating or bland. The movement he started would not have gained such momentum, attracted so many followers, or endured through the centuries otherwise.

What truly unfolds during those one-on-one encounters, intimate healings, and private gatherings with his disciples? And what is happening among the vast crowds that flock just to catch a glimpse of him? These moments must be charged with extraordinary energy and significance.

"Sermon on the Mount," Carl Heinrich Bloch, 1877. This painting depicts Jesus delivering the Sermon on the Mount, as described in the Gospel of Matthew (Chapter 5-7), emphasizing his teachings on humility, compassion, and righteousness, offering a visual representation of his profound words and guidance.

Allen, from the perspective of those who initially encountered him, including the disciples, Jesus seemed to come out of nowhere. Very little was known about him, as we have already established, and he didn't represent himself as being educated and trained in religion. How did he represent himself to the crowds that began to gather around him and with what authority did he represent himself?

Jesus didn't defer a lot to the authority of the fathers or those who came before him. His lectures were without footnotes. He didn't quote a lot of people. When he was asked about the authority in which he did certain things, he said he got it straight from the top.

Jesus talked about God as his father. And that his working in the world was very much like the agency that we see in the relationship between the son and the father. In all traditional societies, the son is really the extension of the father. And in many traditional societies, the son does what the father did.

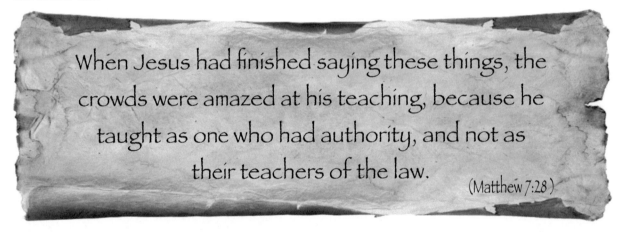

When Jesus had finished saying these things, the crowds were amazed at his teaching, because he taught as one who had authority, and not as their teachers of the law. (Matthew 7:28)

Huston, how did Jesus manage to make his message so compelling and distinct, especially since he was drawing from existing scripture that others were already teaching from?

Jesus spoke with total authority. How is that different? It's the difference between first-hand and second-hand knowledge. The Sufis have a phrase, "There are three ways you can know about fire. The first is hearing about it. There is such a thing as fire. The second is seeing it. And the third is being burned by it. Three degrees of familiarity."

And so it is with truth. We can learn about truth from teachers and others who have been to Istanbul or Delhi or the Taj Mahal. They can tell us and we can see photos of the Taj Mahal. I had seen so many photographs of the time that I thought, okay I know what that looks like. But it wasn't like that at all. It was like a two-dimensional photograph through three-dimensional actuality. And so that's the difference and how the disciples and others heard Jesus. He wasn't quoting what the Torah said. It was as if he were seeing the truth and then becoming transparent to it so it was simply that truth that just came through him to others.

Huston, did Jesus adapt his manner of speaking when imparting teachings to his disciples, who received more extensive instruction from him, in contrast to when he addressed larger crowds?

It is true that all the great teachers rely heavily on metaphor to communicate and Jesus spoke to individuals and crowds mostly in parable. But he says to his disciples I'll tell it to you straight because we have a long-term relationship and have built up some understanding. But to the people out there, if you just lay it on the line propositionally like that, it's gonna roll off of them like water off of a duck's back. And it's the artistry of a supreme teacher to be able to know where those pores and those crevices and the armor that a human being develops lies and move in to those pores in a way that can really reach their hearts.

Allen, what would you consider to be Jesus' go-to rhetorical tool when responding to someone, the one he used most often and to the greatest effect?

Jesus had a reputation for responding to people verbally in several ways. One was to use a metaphor or an image from lived reality, from the kitchen, from housework, from farm work, from fishing. That's because that is what people knew, and he could relate to that. He related to it because he was one of them. There are images that are attributed to him that are very evocative, and were probably even more evocative in his time than they are now because most of us who are reading are not from an agrarian population. Some of the richness of it is lost on us. Subsequent readership of city slickers like it, but don't completely understand it.

Richard, metaphors must resonate across diverse audiences, and Jesus, addressing people from varied backgrounds in terms of class, profession, education, religion, ethnicity, and culture, exemplified this skill. How did he effectively communicate to such a wide spectrum of individuals?

His images are more often images from the kitchen, from nature, from the domestic home, flowers in the field. Because he's not teaching in the world of formal religion. He doesn't talk with academic clerical vocabulary. He talks with the vocabulary of the underclass, if you will. The vocabulary of housewives and working men. And he uses the images of things that they would understand and see every day. That really is very consoling to me. Because it tells me that religion and life are one thing.

Allen, Father Rohr commented that Jesus doesn't talk with academic clerical vocabulary. He says Jesus talks with the vocabulary of the "underclass." Could you comment on that?

The language of Jesus is compelling for us because on one level, it appears so simple. Homespun, is how some people have described it. He uses agrarian metaphors. He makes reference to things that are common. Things that people encounter regularly in the contemporary world. He doesn't invest those things with a transcendent quality. He helps us to see the transcendence in those things.

When we look at the harvest, when we look at the rain, when we look at the sun, when we look at the birds in the air, the flowers in the field, we can see the goodness of God in these things. The very existence of the world as it is, testifies to the goodness of God.

Huston, what is it about nature that informs so much of Jesus' language?

Virgin nature is probably our clearest aperture to the heart. It's even better than great art, whether it be the Hallelujah Chorus or an icon even. Religious art is a great help in accessing the Spirit,

Then he told them many things in parables, saying: "A farmer went out to sow his seed. As he was scattering the seed, some fell along the path, and the birds came and ate it up. Some fell on rocky places, where it did not have much soil. It sprang up quickly, because the soil was shallow. But when the sun came up, the plants were scorched, and they withered because they had no root. Other seed fell among thorns, which grew up and choked the plants. Still other seed fell on good soil, where it produced a crop—a hundred, sixty or thirty times what was sown. Whoever has ears, let them hear." (Matthew 13:3-9)

"The Sower," painted by Vincent Willem van Gogh in 1888. This painting portrays a figure scattering seeds in a field, reminiscent of the Parable of the Sower from the Gospel of Matthew (Chapter 13), symbolizing the dissemination of spiritual truth and the potential for transformative growth.

but it doesn't do it to the extent. I'll just give you one example here. Once I was in at a conference with over a hundred people. It was on the Pacific coast and the dining room looked out over the ocean. As we were eating, the sun began to set. The closer as it disappeared, more and more over the horizon, why, the conversation stopped. Even the good food and the conversation. People were just glued to that. And when the final little sliver disappeared a three-year-old kid started to applaud, and the whole dining room picked up. I mean God, you've done it again. What a show this is. And that's the power of nature, and especially virgin nature.

Huston, we see how important metaphor was and how it aided Jesus in getting across his point. What was the rhetorical style in which he delivered his message whether through parable or direct language?

Somebody has given the phrase, Gigantesque, to Jesus' language. You know there are times when the impact of whatever it is we're experiencing is so powerful that normal language just doesn't convey the feeling. And we reach out desperately for the superlative and even change the language a little bit to get across the point. This isn't the way you are talking about happiness. This is of a different order of magnitude. So let's call it blessedness rather than happiness.

Let's just take the mad side of it. "Leave everything you have and follow me." Oh boy, that is taking a plunge. And "Unless you deny yourself and take up your cross?" The cross was the most brutal, agonizing form of death in Jesus' time. Isn't it pretty mad, crazy, to ask people to voluntarily submit themselves to the most agonizing form of a torturous death? "It is easier for a camel to pass through a needle's eye than for a rich man to enter into the kingdom." I mean, if you try to visualize this it's crazy. So that is what we find just interlacing Jesus' words

Allen, in diving into the actual style Jesus employed when speaking, particularly to larger crowds, Huston Smith mentioned the term 'Gigantesque,' implying that it sometimes involved exaggeration for emphasis and impact. Can you shed some light on how Jesus employed this technique?

As you know, we often exaggerate a point, to drive it home. And I think there's something of that in the language of Jesus. It's colorful language. As any preacher knows, it doesn't help to bore people. Sometimes their eyes are open, but they were asleep in those pews. You got to wake them up. And he was good at that.

At another level there's indirection. He had a reputation for being indirect. For being cagey in his language. In modern scholarship, this has been explained by saying that Jesus perpetrated what one scholar referred to as "the messianic secret." That is that Jesus was the messiah, but he didn't want anybody to know it, at least not during his lifetime.

But I think we can put a more fruitful spin on that, or something that helps to clarify what was really going on in Jesus' discourse, and that's this; Jesus was moving people by what he was saying. He was drawing attention to himself. And in this context, in the political context, that's very dangerous. He's moving masses of people. He's having an effect on them. And he has to be careful when he talks.

We know from other kinds of folklore of subjugated people who are under oppression or domination at various times one of the devices that they use for communicating with each other is indirect language. Jesus is in a highly charged, politically problematic, dangerous situation. So he's not going to lay his cards on the table all the time. And he's going to say things and wink. He knows what he's talking about. The people know what he's talking about. He knows they know. They know he knows. So there's a lot of communication going on there that's not being spoken. There's a lot of things going on between the lines. And we have to know how the metaphors play out. The gaps that we see, the indirection, the caginess.

Jesus realizes that his situation is perilous and he's not going to say the first thing that comes to his mind every time. Some people need to know, some people don't need to know. He speaks to both audiences at the same time. So his language is going to be unusual at times.

Huston, religion at the time, and to a significant degree today, has been to explain its respective principles and, more often than not, how they should be practiced and followed. Jesus didn't seem to follow that conventional template. Could you elaborate on that?

Jesus didn't put the emphasis on telling people what to do. The emphasis was putting it up to the listener. What do you want to make with your life? On this decision you're facing, do you want to go on the left-hand fork, or the right-hand fork?

"Sermon on Mount (detail)," 19th Century, by Henrik Olrik. This detail possibly captures a scene from the Sermon on the Mount, depicted in the Gospel of Matthew (Chapter 5-7), showcasing Jesus teaching his disciples and the crowd, offering moral and spiritual guidance that resonates through generations.

"Tribute Money," 1886-1894, by James Tissot. This painting depicts the scene from the Gospel of Matthew (Chapter 22, verses 15-22) where Jesus distinguishes between terrestrial and divine authority, evading a trap set by his hostile audience as they listen intently to his response.

Putting it that way so that it would almost require a response from the hearer rather than if you simply told them and at best you might think, well, I learned something and that might be useful. But it doesn't have the carryover and the impact that the invitational approach does.

Allen, many individuals who encountered Jesus, whether individually or in crowds, often disagreed with his interpretation of scripture. They frequently challenged him, sometimes in a forceful or even aggressive manner. How was Jesus able to maintain his composure and either defuse the situation or, in many cases, redirect the discourse?

We have a number of different kinds of public personalities from this period. We have records of them. Their public speech. And if you were going to be any kind of itinerating public intellectual with your own spin on things, or your own kind of social critique, one of the things you needed to have in your discursive toolbox was a capacity for one-liners. You had to be able to say things to put the hecklers in their place. You also had to be able to discern a question which wasn't really a question.

See, there are people who ask questions not to get certain answers, but to incriminate the people to whom the question was addressed. There's a classic case of this in gospel traditions where somebody asks Jesus should we pay taxes to Caesar or not? You're talking about this kingdom. I mean, we don't have to pay taxes to anybody. God is our king. So, should we pay taxes to Caesar or not?

The Roman coin Denarius of Tiberius most likely the one Jesus was referring to in Matthew 22:15-22.

Now, this is just a no-win situation. By this time he's got a public following of people who believe that he really is, in some way, the agent bringing about the Kingdom of God. And they know, among other things, that means political autonomy for Israel. Throwing off the yoke of Roman domination. So if he says, yeah, pay your taxes, then all of that juice is squandered and he loses that credibility with the people, with the masses. If he says, no don't pay your taxes, that's a death sentence. He may as well just call up the police and give them his address.

So what does he do? He gives an answer that's not an answer that goes down into history as one of the best one-liners of all time. Or one of the greatest sort of wise-guy responses of all time. "You have a coin? Let me take a look at it. Whose face is on it? It's Caesar's. Give to Caesar what's Caesar's. Give to God what belongs to God." There's no comeback to that. So that one goes down in gospel tradition and into history.

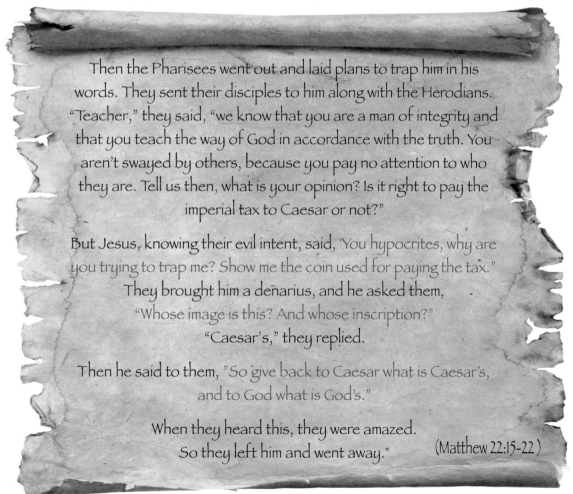

Then the Pharisees went out and laid plans to trap him in his words. They sent their disciples to him along with the Herodians. "Teacher," they said, "we know that you are a man of integrity and that you teach the way of God in accordance with the truth. You aren't swayed by others, because you pay no attention to who they are. Tell us then, what is your opinion? Is it right to pay the imperial tax to Caesar or not?"

But Jesus, knowing their evil intent, said, "You hypocrites, why are you trying to trap me? Show me the coin used for paying the tax." They brought him a denarius, and he asked them, "Whose image is this? And whose inscription?"

"Caesar's," they replied.

Then he said to them, "So give back to Caesar what is Caesar's, and to God what is God's."

When they heard this, they were amazed. So they left him and went away." (Matthew 22:15-22)

If you were going to be that kind of person, if you were going to be in the public like that, you had to be able to come up with the sound bite that was going to do the job for you. And if you couldn't do that, then you went to the dustbin of history with all the other people who couldn't do it. This was one of the things that he could do. There were several things that he could do that really qualified him for this role. And apparently he did them very well. People remembered him.

Reflections

Without establishing authority, your words will have little meaning to a discerning audience. Given the importance and power of Jesus' message, this was something he required from day one. So where did Jesus get this authority? As Allen said, "His lectures were without footnotes. He didn't quote a lot of people." Jesus pulled no punches. Up front, he steadfastly asserted that his authority came straight from the top—God. There were no intermediaries. His clear and undiluted message served as a direct link to truth and the source. That will get any audience to sit up and take notice.

> "For I have not spoken on my own authority, but the Father who sent me has himself given me a commandment—what to say and what to speak."
>
> (John 12:49-50)

But what kept the crowds coming back for more, particularly in the beginning when he was an unknown with no following? How could such a revolutionary message penetrate the walls of even the most cynical or disbelieving? Not all, but enough to ignite his movement. I believe it was because, as Huston described it, "It was as if he were seeing the truth and then again becoming transparent to it. So it was simply that truth that just came through him to others."

Encountering such a message was not a passive experience; it affected people in real-time. Some were filled with joy and hope, others harbored doubts or reacted with disbelief, while still others responded with ridicule or even anger. To be sure, it provoked introspection, challenged long-held beliefs, and, in many cases, changed people's understanding of the world and their place within it. He got their attention.

Having pronounced his authority, whether accepted or not, my next line of inquiry was the actual language he used. What, aside from the proclamation that he was getting his information straight from the top, was so compelling that you'd stick around for the second or third act? Based on my understanding of the Gospels, supported by my interviews for the film, and most importantly my years absorbing the teachings of Joseph Campbell, I understood it had to be related to Jesus' use of metaphor and parable.

Jesus explained to his disciples that he spoke plainly to them because of their close relationship and deeper understanding. However, to the general public, speaking directly would be ineffective, as it would be like "water off a duck's back" as Huston put it. A supreme teacher knows how to penetrate the defenses people build and reach their hearts.

Jesus, being a masterful teacher, knows that speaking plainly to his disciples works because they have a solid rapport and understanding. But when addressing the masses, Jesus opts for parables and metaphors drawn from everyday life—things like farming or household chores—because they are relatable. Jesus deliberately avoids using formal religious language, instead favoring the everyday words of ordinary people.

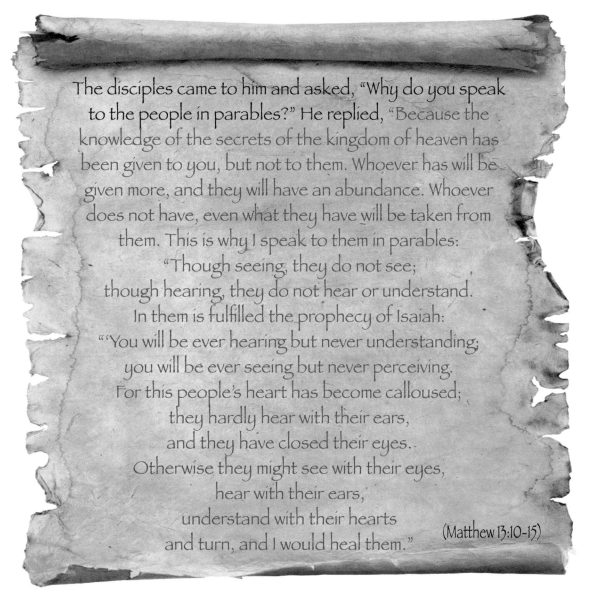

The disciples came to him and asked, "Why do you speak to the people in parables?" He replied, "Because the knowledge of the secrets of the kingdom of heaven has been given to you, but not to them. Whoever has will be given more, and they will have an abundance. Whoever does not have, even what they have will be taken from them. This is why I speak to them in parables:
"Though seeing, they do not see;
though hearing, they do not hear or understand.
In them is fulfilled the prophecy of Isaiah:
"'You will be ever hearing but never understanding;
you will be ever seeing but never perceiving.
For this people's heart has become calloused;
they hardly hear with their ears,
and they have closed their eyes.
Otherwise they might see with their eyes,
hear with their ears,
understand with their hearts
and turn, and I would heal them.'"

(Matthew 13:10-15)

"Peaceable Kingdom," 1833–1834, Edward Hicks. This painting depicts a serene scene of animals and children coexisting peacefully, symbolizing the prophetic vision of universal harmony and peace found in Isaiah 11:6-9. This scene reflects the biblical prophecy where the wolf will live with the lamb, and a little child will lead them, representing the ultimate fulfillment of God's kingdom and the peace that comes through Jesus.

This approach highlights the connection between spirituality and daily life. His use of simple language isn't just about accessibility; it is about encouraging people to see the divine in the ordinary. By referencing common things like harvests or birds, Jesus invites his listeners to recognize the beauty and goodness of the world as evidence of God's presence.

Jesus connects with them because he is one of them. As Allen relates, his evocative imagery, drawn from the common experiences of his time, might lose some richness for modern readers who are less familiar with agrarian life. Yet, his use of simple, everyday language—from nature, domestic life, and work—resonates deeply. As Huston puts it, "Nature is our clearest aperture to the divine." Jesus doesn't use academic or clerical jargon but speaks in the language of housewives and working men, making his teachings accessible and relatable. This blend of religion and everyday life is consoling, showing that the sacred is intertwined with the mundane.

Jesus also uses bold and provocative language. His messages hint at a deeper, perhaps even radical, meaning behind his words. Instead of settling for ordinary expressions, he elevates his language to convey profound truths. And as Huston describes, his language is often "gigantesque." Jesus' deliberate use of exaggerated and colorful language also serves to engage and challenge his audience, disrupting their usual ways of thinking and prompting deeper reflection. By avoiding conventional speech and embracing a more unconventional style, he may have sought to shake people out of complacency and provoke them to consider alternative perspectives. This method of communication may have subtly hinted at a deeper, more radical purpose behind his teachings, challenging societal norms and inviting listeners to question the status quo.

Huston also observes another striking aspect of Jesus' approach: the radical demands he makes, challenging people to leave everything behind and follow him or to take up their cross as a symbol of extreme commitment and sacrifice. His use of provocative imagery, like a camel passing through the eye of a needle to illustrate the difficulty for the rich to enter God's kingdom, carries a subversive edge, pushing listeners to reconsider their values and priorities.

Allen highlights that Jesus has a reputation for being indirect and cagey in his language, a deliberate strategy reflecting his awareness of the political and social dangers of his time. In my interview, he noted that scholars often describe this as the "messianic secret," suggesting that Jesus knows he is the Messiah but chooses not to openly declare it to avoid premature and potentially dangerous reactions from authorities.

Jesus spoke all these things to the crowd in parables; he did not say anything to them without using a parable. So was fulfilled what was spoken through the prophet: "I will open my mouth in parables, I will utter things hidden since the creation of the world."

(Matthew 13:34-35)

In the politically charged atmosphere under Roman occupation, Jesus' teachings are powerful and influential, necessitating careful communication. His effective use of metaphors and parables allows him to speak truth to power without directly provoking it, ensuring his safety and that of his followers. This approach is vividly demonstrated in his handling of the Pharisees when asked about paying Roman taxes.

Jesus' language is designed to be understood by those ready to receive his deeper truths while remaining obscure to others. This selective revelation protects his mission, allowing him to influence and mobilize his followers while minimizing the risk of immediate backlash from those who might seek to silence him.

"The Baptism of Christ," 1622-1623, Guido Reni. This painting depicts John the Baptist baptizing Jesus in the River Jordan, symbolizing the beginning of Jesus' public ministry and the moment when the Holy Spirit descends upon him, as described in Matthew 3:16-17. This scene highlights the divine affirmation of Jesus as God's Son and serves as a powerful representation of spiritual cleansing and rebirth.

"I will utter things hidden...." IV

Matthew 13:35

Jesus' teachings are characterized by their richness, complexity, and multi-layered nature, presenting profound challenges to those who encounter them. Born and raised in a Jewish family, Jesus was deeply immersed in the cultural and religious traditions of Judaism. Despite this background, his teachings often diverged from the traditional religious views prevalent in his time. I am eager to explore the factors that lead to this apparent contradiction and understand the underlying motivations behind Jesus' departure from conventional religious norms.

In a similar vein, I am interested in why Jesus is often seen as an establishment religious figure today when what we read in the Gospels depicts a much more subversive teacher—one that became seen as such a threat to the religious and secular powers of his time that it eventually led to his execution.

Jesus most often refers to himself as the "Son of Man." I am extremely interested in uncovering the significance of this title and how it reflects his identity and mission. I find it fascinating that he emphasized his humanity so much, yet many have elevated him to a "divine pedestal." How has this shift affected our understanding of his core messages?

I am also curious about the ways different cultures and denominations have interpreted Jesus' teachings to fit their own traditions and social agendas, and how these interpretations might have diverged from what Jesus actually said and did. For example, why do mainstream Christian practices often focus on issues like sexual morality, which Jesus seldom addressed, rather than his emphasis on compassion, nonviolence, and simplicity? Regarding compassion, I also want to understand how he emphasized this quality in his teachings over the rigid religious rules that were such a focus of the temple cult in his time.

Finally, I want to better understand Jesus' perspective on failure and success, and how these views influence his broader teachings on spirituality and living in the present. This aspect of his message, emphasizing the importance of vulnerability and letting go, is often overlooked by mainstream churches. How do these values of embracing failure and living in the moment fit into the larger framework of his teachings, and why have they been so frequently ignored in traditional religious practices?

Richard, why do you think people today often misunderstand the true nature of Jesus' teachings and role within the context of his time? What don't we get?

It sometimes surprises people that Jesus would be considered, in any way, subversive because we've made him so much the founder of our saved religion, that we think of him very much as an establishment man. But if you actually are honest about the content of his teaching and the context of his teaching, he's almost undercutting every normal expectation of what religion is supposed to be. If you were going to create a founder of a religion, you would never have picked Jesus.

Jesus must be the most misused, misquoted, misunderstood man in human history. And I don't think that's an exaggeration. It seems that he's been used by every culture to prop them up, to hold them together, by every denomination, to make him say what we want him to say. By empires because we needed a God figure and he was the available God figure for Europeans. In many ways it didn't matter what he really said. It's what we wanted him to say. And what we found out is that many people really thought he said these things that they presumed they wanted him to say.

So the easiest thing to do is just ignore the scriptures and create a religion of devotions and various exercises that are nice and spiritual, but have little to do with the message of Jesus. And from the Protestant tradition, what was more common, was to call ourselves a very biblical tradition, while in fact ignoring seven eighths of what Jesus said. I'm not saying that in criticism of any particular denomination, because I think, frankly, Jesus is too much for the human psyche. We almost have to whittle him down to handle. I don't know that any of us are capable of receiving the whole message. So I have created Jesus in my own image that I can relate to. Instead of conventional wisdom, I think it's very fair to say that the teaching of Jesus is much more subversive wisdom.

Huston, how did Jesus employ personal and familial imagery to express the notion that his followers were regarded as the children of God?

Jesus preached that you are the children of God. Now that's very personalistic imagery which came very naturally to him. In our jaded and secular time, it doesn't sit very well. But really, the parent-child relationship at its best, is maybe the most precious relationship that there is. My wife and I see it now with our youngest grandson, who's only five years old. Nothing is more important than that original bonding, because that feeds basic trust into the life. And if that's not there, like learning a language you recover it with very chancy success. So it was that sense of calling them in very personalistic language to the divinity that is within them.

Richard, what does Jesus' use of the term "Son of Man" reveal about how he viewed his own identity and mission, and how has the historical inclination to idolize figures, such as Jesus, influenced our interaction with and understanding of their teachings?

The most common word that Jesus uses to describe himself is the term usually translated by Christians with capital letters, "Son of Man." We now know that it didn't have to be capitalized. It most certainly wasn't originally and that very likely he was calling himself Everyman, the human being. The son of humanity. He was talking as the quintessential human being. He refers to himself in the four gospels by this term 79 times. No other term even comes close to that. Jesus doesn't go around calling himself God. But we quickly pedestalized him, put him up as a God figure, and lost what was the primary lure or attraction, which was that he was the quintessential human being. This is what it means to be a full human being.

"Christ and the Children," painted in 1910 by Emil Nolde. This painting depicts Jesus surrounded by children, evoking the biblical narrative from the Gospel of Matthew (Chapter 19, verses 13-15), where Jesus welcomes children and emphasizes the importance of childlike faith and innocence in the kingdom of God.

For some reason it is very effective to avoid what a person is really saying to you by flattering them. Flattery actually pushes the person away, puts them up on a pedestal, so you don't have to really engage with them. I believe, historically, we have done this with Jesus. We have pedestalized him, quickly worshiped him as God, and it gave us a very effective way to avoid what he was really talking about. And it works. If you worship the messenger, you can, for some reason, avoid the message. And if you look at Jesus, his words to his disciples are always, follow me, not worship me.

And yet most of Christian services are preoccupied with worshiping Jesus. He's saying, follow me. Do what I'm doing. Come and live the way I'm living. A simple life in this world. A shared life in this world. A non violent life. A compassionate life. And I don't think we did this consciously. I think it's simply the nature of the ego.

If we can avoid surrender, we'll find some way to do it. And Jesus' whole message is about vulnerability. So we found a way to avoid his vulnerable message by making him God. Now I, as a Christian, believe in the divinity of Jesus Christ. But I think that's something you've got to come to through experiencing the depth of his humanity. And when you too quickly say Jesus is Lord before the Spirit has led you there and taught you that in the depths of your experience in your own heart, it usually is pushing Jesus away. In the name of loving Jesus. In the name of worshipping him, you can stop following him.

"Christ Pantocrator Icon, Saint Catherine's Monastery, Mount Sinai," 6th Century, Unknown Artist. This painting depicts Christ as the ruler and judge of the universe, with one hand raised in blessing and the other holding the Gospels, symbolizing his divine authority and his role as both savior and judge, as described in John 5:22-23.

Richard, how do you perceive the disconnection between the teachings of Jesus as portrayed in the four gospels and the topics that seem to dominate modern Christianity?

We've largely projected onto Jesus what we want him to say, and therefore we think he must have really said it. But you go to the four gospels and he didn't talk about most of the things Christianity is preoccupied with today. And in fact, you could make the statement even stronger that the things we are preoccupied with he never talked about, and the things he did talk about, like non-violence and simplicity of lifestyle, have been consistently ignored by most of the mainline churches.

The example I always use in this age of republican family values is I know as a priest, many times I've looked for the proper readings for Holy Family Sunday. And it's real hard to find any in the New Testament, at least in the four Gospels any example where Jesus is really pushing mother and daddy and children and white picket fence. In fact, there's not a single one.

I think what most people want religion for is basically for social order. They want religion for the sake of social control. We need that to hold the neighborhood together. To hold a family system together. That's a very worthwhile goal. But it isn't what God came to earth for. Not for the sake of social order or social control, but for divine union.

Jesus never goes down the path of what I'm going to call conventional wisdom. He never points out the shadowy things that we're all afraid of, the so-called hot sins. He never seems to worry about the hot sins. The gambling and the sex and the dancing and the drinking, which some denominations think is the heart of the matter. For him, it's the issues of power, prestige, illusion, and blindness. This concern for prestige that basically blinds you to what is real and what is true and what is good and what is beautiful.

Huston, what core message do you believe Jesus conveyed regarding the prioritization of compassion over rigid adherence to laws and regulations?

Jesus placed the emphasis clearly on the "politics of compassion." Put compassion above legalistic observances. He cut through those laws. He didn't dishonor them. He simply said if you live your life legalistically, in terms of these laws, you're neglecting what is most important, namely compassionate behavior towards everyone.

The conventional wisdom involved living up to rules. Don't do this, don't do that. Don't do the other thing, and then the positive, do this, love the Lord your God with all your heart, and so on. That was the conventional religion. And in the face of that, Jesus placed the emphasis on the religion of the heart, which involves above all else love of neighbor and trying to treat the neighbor, in the words of the Apostle Paul in Romans, "Rejoice with those who rejoice; mourn with those who mourn," which is a shorthand way of saying feel their feelings as if they were your own.

54

That was the new note, but it was a matter of emphasis, not a clean-cut rejection of his Jewish heritage. Hillel was asked to summarize the whole of the Torah, the Old Testament, while standing on one foot. They asked for that because they were in terrible circumstances and they wanted a mantra that compressed the whole heritage of the Torah into a phrase. He said, "What is hateful to you, do not do to your neighbor. That is the whole Torah; the rest is commentary. Go and learn." Later Christians were going to develop the Jesus prayer from that. A phrase that you just keep going like a mantra. He said, "Thou shalt love your neighbor as yourself."

If you take it in terms of specific teaching I'll go so far as to say there's nothing new in Christ's teaching. It was the emphasis, and more important than the emphasis, the way he himself lived out this different emphasis. And if it's just emphasis but still the same issues, how did so much come from that friction? With the establishment, the difference of emphasis in itself caused conflict.

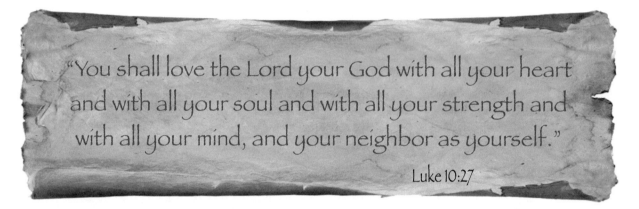

"You shall love the Lord your God with all your heart and with all your soul and with all your strength and with all your mind, and your neighbor as yourself."

Luke 10:27

Richard, what fundamental shift in perspective does Jesus' teachings advocate regarding the nature of religious practice, emphasizing relationship over mere adherence to rules or requirements?

I think it's crucial to understand Jesus is not primarily talking about a system of requirements. A behavioral set of patterns that will make God like you. It's not a religion of requirements, it's a religion of relationship. Relationship is everything. Right relationship. It's how to be present. How to be vulnerable. How to let other people change you. It's all about relationships. But the school of relationships is a much more demanding school. You have to grow up. You have to change. You have to forgive. You have to let go. I have to let you be right once in a while.

That is too hard. So we made it into a pseudo-hard thing called requirements. And every denomination chooses what they're going to be upset about. Drinking or smoking or dancing, none of which Jesus talked about. Usually, sexual sins, which Jesus hardly ever talked about. The issues of Jesus are violence and greed. Clearly, violence and greed. Which anthropologists say, undoubtedly, are the two things that will destroy the world. It's self-evident once you hear that.

"The Good Samaritan," painted in 1890 by Vincent Willem van Gogh. This painting depicts the biblical parable of the Good Samaritan, illustrating the compassionate act of helping a wounded stranger, as recounted in the Gospel of Luke (Chapter 10, verses 25-37), highlighting themes of love, kindness, and the importance of caring for others regardless of differences.

And if anyone's a great spiritual teacher they're going to have very clear taboos against violence and against greed.

The Sermon on the Mount is entirely about living a simple life in this world and a non-violent life. We simply weren't ready for it. I'm told that the very word nonviolence did not even exist in the major languages of the West until the 1960s. The very word. Because it wasn't in our concept. We weren't ready to believe such impossible teachings.

Jesus is concerned much more about the present than the future, but it's much harder to live in the present than to idealize some game of crime and punishment. And that's what most denominational religion is. It's all crime and punishment. It's a big, gigantic police system, and we priests are supposed to be the police keeping you all in line. Jesus refuses to be a divine policeman because that isn't his issue. It's not about some requirements that create a wonderful future, but it's about what's right here, right now. And if you get it now you get it. Who you are now, what you choose now. I think, Jesus is saying, you will be forever.

Huston, when considering the historical context of Jesus' teachings, particularly within the religious landscape of ancient Palestine, how might his message have been perceived as a unique alternative amidst prevalent cultural practices, and how does this perspective extend to broader human history?

If you take a historical look at it, which is always appropriate, he was giving his message to a very small circle. In the Palestine of those days, it wasn't religion's most glorious moment. I mean, fertility rites with orgies and things like that. And so, for his audience, given the other options that were around, and honoring his Jewish heritage as he did, it may have been an absolutely accurate, straightforward statement that among the options that your cultures are giving you, this is the only way.

If you take that and expand it for human history, we're in a very different ballgame. But if anybody wants to ignore that and assume that Jesus was speaking for all time and all places who did not know about Buddha and Muhammad who came later, then I would say that the way Christians picked up that statement was providential. Because "No one cometh to the Father save through the Son," has four levels of meaning. One is the historical Jesus who walked the paths of the hills of Galilee. If you have to go through that Jesus, good luck! That Jesus was gone by about 30 or 33 A.D.

There is The Risen Christ as well. And in order not to prolong this, I'm going to go straight for the top one which comes in the first four verses of the book of John which begins "In the beginning was the word." The Greek for that is logos, which is a much more voluminous protean

"Christ Taking Leave of the Apostles (detail of Siena Cathedral altarpiece)," created in 1311 by Duccio di Buoninsegna. This detail depicts the biblical scene from the Gospel of John (Chapter 14, verse 6), where Jesus declares, "I am the way and the truth and the life. No one comes to the Father except through me," emphasizing Jesus' central role as the mediator between humanity and God, depicted within the larger context of his farewell discourse to his apostles.

word than we think of letters. That didn't mean that in the beginning was the logos, and the logos was God, and the logos was with God in the beginning. Then it goes on to say, "And nothing was made except through the Logos. Now, the Logos became flesh. But listen to that first part. Nothing was made except through the Logos. That means Buddha, from a Christian point of view, wasn't made except through the Logos. When you raise the Logos as what you have to come through, that really opens the arms to anything in this universe being an entrée to the Father.

"Christ and the Woman Taken in Adultery," painted in 1644 by Rembrandt van Rijn. This painting depicts the biblical scene from the Gospel of John (Chapter 8, verses 1-11), where Jesus forgives a woman caught in adultery, illustrating themes of compassion, forgiveness, and the transformative power of grace.

Richard, how do you perceive Jesus' approach of challenging individuals to exceed their limits while also demonstrating complete acceptance and love for them if they were to fall short?

Jesus would simultaneously push people to their best, maybe push them beyond what they were ready to hear, but accept them totally. That's an art form, to know how to do both. You can't fake it. You've got to love the person. You've got to honestly love the person or you can't do that.

Probably the clearest example of where he did that was the woman caught in adultery. He refuses to shame her. He refuses to let anybody else shame her. "Neither do I condemn you," he said. But don't do this anymore. It's not gonna work. It's not gonna get you anywhere. This is not your best self. So she must have felt his protection, his embrace, his forgiveness, his unconditional acceptance of her. But at the same time, he is pushing her. Don't do this, you know. This isn't gonna get you anywhere. It's not gonna work.

That would probably be one of the clearest, concise examples of his simultaneously embracing and challenging the same person. But once you get it, you see that he's doing that all the time. And again, I think you can only give away what you've become. You can only treat people how you really feel about them. If you don't really love them, if you don't really respect them, you won't know how to achieve that paradox and that balance. Obviously, Jesus did.

> "Let any one of you who is without sin be the first to throw a stone at her." Then he stoops down and continues writing on the ground.
>
> One by one, starting with the oldest, the accusers leave until Jesus is left alone with the woman. He asks her where her accusers are and if anyone has condemned her. When she responds that no one has condemned her, Jesus declares, "Then neither do I condemn you. Go now and leave your life of sin."
>
> John 8:7-11

Richard, how do you interpret the role of failure as a profound instructor in spiritual growth, and how does it prompt individuals to reevaluate their sources of identity and success?

Success has almost nothing to teach you after 30. All you need is a few successes to get started.

To give yourself a sense of identity, and know, I'm okay, and I can do a few things right. Now I like successes. They still feel good, but they don't teach me anything anymore. Failure is the great teacher, and all your great spiritual wisdom figures will say that. That failure pulls from beneath you what you're relying upon. So you have to rely on something deeper. It pulls the rug out from beneath you. You have to say, what is my success? What is my identity? What is my name? What is my security? And unless you're forced to ask that question, at an ever deeper level, you simply don't grow spiritually. You don't become a larger person. You become a smaller and smaller person. I don't mean to be cynical or negative, but how many older people do we know whose comfort zone is down to two or three friends who are just like them, who have the same prejudices and limited worldviews that they have, and they call that life.

It's all about losing. It's all about not getting your own way. It's about not being in control. And what do you do with that? That's when you become wise. I'm convinced of that. If spirituality is one thing, all great spirituality is about letting go. It's always describing some phenomenon of releasement, forgiveness is the classic word. Do you know two-thirds of Jesus' teaching is directly or indirectly about one thing, forgiveness?

Reflections

Father Rohr succinctly points out that despite our often portraying Jesus as more of an establishment figure, his teachings challenge conventional religious expectations. His message is in stark contrast to the traditional religious practices of his time, emphasizing compassion over legalistic observances and prioritizing relationships over religious requirements. Matthew highlights Jesus' criticism of religious leaders who focus on minor matters while neglecting justice, mercy, and faithfulness.

While the contrast between Jesus' message and that of the Temple Cult was more precise and pronounced in his time, it is hard to argue against the tendency of organized religion throughout history to appropriate and distort Jesus' message to serve various cultural, denominational, and political agendas. We certainly are not immune to this in our time. This speaks to the complexity of interpreting Jesus' teachings and the challenge of fully embracing their radical implications.

Growing up, my experience with Christianity consisted of walking through countless churches and cathedrals in Europe, where my father lived. Because my father (and mother) was a committed atheist, he focused on the history of the church, which in many ways is the history of Europe. The artwork hanging in cathedrals and museums featured depictions almost exclusively of the Christ nature of Jesus. That title, derived from the Greek word "Christos," which translates to the Hebrew "Mashiach" (Messiah), meaning "Anointed One," signified Jesus' role and mission as the chosen one of God.

"Coin in the Fishes Mouth," 1425, Masaccio. This painting depicts the moment when Jesus instructs Peter to find a coin in the mouth of a fish to pay the temple tax, as described in Matthew 17:24-27. This scene illustrates Jesus' divine provision and his teaching on fulfilling civic responsibilities without neglecting spiritual obligations.

"Woe unto you, scribes and Pharisees, hypocrites! for ye pay tithe of mint and anise and cummin, and have omitted the weightier matters of the law, judgment, mercy, and faith: these ought ye to have done, and not to leave the other undone."

(Matthew 17:24-27)

Neither the imagery in Europe nor the church messages I encountered in my twenties focused on Jesus as a person. I had not realized until I came across Father Rohr's work that Jesus often referred to himself as the "Son of Man," highlighting his identification with humanity rather than asserting divine status. This was both revelatory and profound. And this was the side of Jesus I was most interested in exploring in the film. The term, as described by Rohr, underscored Jesus' humanity and solidarity with all people and challenged traditional interpretations by suggesting that Jesus may have intended it to mean "Everyman" or the quintessential human being rather than a divine title.

Jesus' emphasis on his humanity rather than his divinity alone appears radical within the context of organized religion. Its deeper meaning lies in the recognition of Jesus as a model of humanity, emphasizing the fullness and depth of human experience. By highlighting the term "Son of Man" as a symbol of Jesus' humanity, Father Rohr emphasizes the universal aspects of his teachings and the profound implications for understanding human identity and potential. It also encourages us to reconsider our perceptions of Jesus not only as a divine figure but also as a relatable and exemplary human being.

The problem is that Jesus was quickly "pedestalized," held up as a God figure, and we lost what is so attractive about him, which is that he is the "quintessential human being," as Father Rohr refers to him. He points out that by pedestalizing Jesus and his teachings, it becomes easier to avoid engaging with or placing less priority on his actual message. Father Rohr points out that Jesus never said, "Worship me." He said and implied over and over, "Follow me." Jesus calls for discipleship, inviting all he encounters to follow his example rather than idolizing him. Worship, in many ways, can be much easier than following his actual teachings. And his core message, if we look at it honestly, is clear and simple, albeit excruciatingly difficult to realize in all ages. That message is expressed in the "Great Commandment" and is appropriately in red letters.

> "'Love the Lord your God with all your heart and with all your soul and with all your mind.' This is the first and greatest commandment. And the second is like it: 'Love your neighbor as yourself.' All the Law and the Prophets hang on these two commandments."
>
> (Matthew 22:37-39)

Jesus very clearly states that these two commandments encompass the entire Law and the Prophets, suggesting their overarching importance in Christian theology. Two simple yet powerful directives: to love God with all one's being and to love one's neighbor as oneself. While the former emphasizes wholehearted devotion to God, the latter brings clarity and practicality to this divine mandate, making it accessible to all. For me, and likely for many others raised in an environment emphasizing a wrathful, unforgiving God, focusing on "thy neighbor" serves as a bridge between the two commandments. Perhaps, without recognizing it, we connect to the first by focusing on the latter. By centering on "Love your neighbor as yourself," the message becomes remarkably clear in highlighting the interconnectedness of love for God and love for others, suggesting that by embodying love and kindness towards one's neighbor, individuals express their devotion to God in the most tangible and relatable manner. This is why recognizing Jesus as the "quintessential human being" becomes invaluable—he is a man of the people. He is one of us. In essence, focusing on loving one's neighbor simplifies the complexities of religious doctrine, bringing the essence of faith down to its most fundamental and actionable form: to treat others with the same care and respect as one would wish for oneself.

Unfortunately, this simplification poses two very real problems. First and foremost, if we cannot follow even the second commandment, which in a sense fulfills the first, it is clear for all to see—most importantly, ourselves. I have not knowingly been in the presence of a saint—canonized or otherwise—and I believe they might be the few who checked those boxes. A simple test like the Great Commandment indicts us all.

""The Pharisees Question Jesus," 1886–1894, James Tissot. This painting depicts the Pharisees questioning Jesus, attempting to trap him with their inquiries, as described in Matthew 22:15-22. This scene illustrates the challenges Jesus faced from religious leaders and highlights his wisdom and authority in responding to their attempts to undermine his teachings.

"The Pilgrim of the Cross at the End of His Journey," 1846-1848, Thomas Cole. Two young men each begin a pilgrimage—one to the cross and the other through the world. The route to the cross is mountainous and difficult, while the pathway through the world tempts with a beautiful valley. By the end of their journeys, the pilgrim of the cross discovers the bright light and angels of redemption, but the pilgrim of the world finds only a wasteland of emptiness and fear.

Perhaps that is why Jesus proclaimed, "But small the gate and narrow the road that leads to life and only a few find it." (John 7:14). This is my favorite verse in one sense because it is an ever-present wake-up call and because it reminds me that we all fall short.

The second problem in Jesus' time and even today is that organized religion has made the entirety of Jesus' teachings into highly complex theology in need of a highly trained temple cult to break it down to the masses who are ignorant of the ways of God. Well, if the law is so simple, why do we need a temple cult and all of the attendant problems inherent in any large and powerful institution? With these two simple commandments, Jesus turns the whole system on its head, honoring that people are very complex and therefore making the law very simple.

Father Rohr builds on this when he describes Jesus' emphasis on our need to shift from a religion of requirements to a religion of relationship. This challenges the notion of religion as a set of behavioral patterns to appease God, instead asserting the primacy of authentic relationship and right living in the present moment. Highlighting the demands of true relationship—such as growth, change, forgiveness, and vulnerability—invites his followers to move beyond superficial adherence to rules towards a deeper engagement with the complexities of human connection.

As Huston Smith explains, Jesus focuses on the "religion of the heart," centered on genuine love and empathy toward others. By emphasizing the importance of compassion and empathy, Jesus challenges individuals to move beyond superficial acts of piety toward authentic relationships and solidarity with those in need. What goes hand in glove with loving thy neighbor is forgiveness, which occupies a central role in Jesus' teachings, reflecting his emphasis on reconciliation and release. As Father Rohr points out, two-thirds of Jesus' teaching was directly or indirectly about one thing: forgiveness. Forgiveness liberates individuals from resentment and facilitates spiritual growth, embodying the essence of divine love and mercy.

As someone who knows from experience that my failures have taught me much more than my successes, it is heartening to see in Jesus' teachings an emphasis on the transformative potential of failure, in which he encourages individuals to learn and grow from setbacks. The Gospel of Luke highlights the paradox of losing one's life to find it.

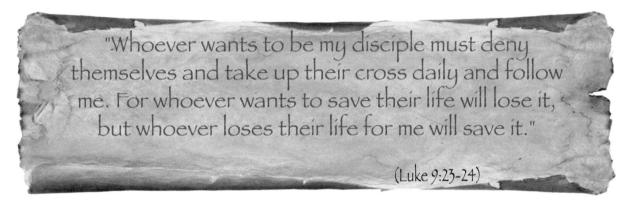

"Whoever wants to be my disciple must deny themselves and take up their cross daily and follow me. For whoever wants to save their life will lose it, but whoever loses their life for me will save it."

(Luke 9:23-24)

What stands out in this passage is its profound insight into the transformative power of failure and the necessity of letting go for spiritual growth. As Father Rohr points out, it is through failure that one is compelled to confront questions of identity, security, and purpose, fostering inner growth and resilience. He interprets failure as an opportunity for self-reflection and expansion, challenging individuals to move beyond their comfort zones and confront their limitations. Rohr emphasizes the significance of losing gracefully and relinquishing control, pointing to Jesus' themes of humility, surrender, and forgiveness that are also found in many spiritual traditions. He suggests that true wisdom and spiritual maturity are cultivated through the willingness to confront failure, embrace vulnerability, and let go of ego-driven desires.

Staying with this theme, Father Rohr points out that Jesus' approach is to simultaneously challenge and accept individuals, highlighting the delicate balance between pushing someone to their best while also offering unconditional love and acceptance when we all fall short. Jesus' refusal to shame the woman caught in adultery and offer her forgiveness and acceptance exemplifies the essence of unconditional love. However, he also challenges her to recognize and change her behavior, guiding her toward a path of growth and transformation. Ultimately, his ability to simultaneously embrace and challenge individuals speaks to his profound understanding of human nature and his commitment to guiding others toward their best selves with compassion and integrity.

When the teachers of the law who were Pharisees saw him eating with the sinners and tax collectors, they asked his disciples: "Why does he eat with tax collectors and sinners?" On hearing this, Jesus said to them, "It is not the healthy who need a doctor, but the sick. I have not come to call the righteous, but sinners." (Mark 2:13-17)

Why do you eat and drink with sinners?

Luke 5:30

In this section of the film, I explore an important aspect of Jesus' ministry—his affinity for those whom society often neglects or marginalizes. I want to understand why Jesus consistently aligns himself with the powerless, the outcasts, and the "sinners," and how this choice challenges the established social norms of his time.

I am particularly curious about the significance of Jesus' social interactions, especially his participation in meals and gatherings that seem unconventional for a religious leader. What is the deeper meaning behind Jesus attending these "parties" and breaking traditional purity laws? How do these actions convey his message of radical inclusivity?

Another area I wish to delve into is Jesus' use of metaphors and parables. How does he use the imagery of meals and banquets to illustrate the Kingdom of God? What can we learn from his teachings that depict divine love as an inclusive, all-encompassing embrace?

Finally, I seek to understand the prophetic tradition that Jesus draws from, which emphasizes the restoration and inclusion of all, especially the socially and ritually unclean. How does this tradition influence his ministry and resonate with those experiencing marginalization?

In summary, through this section of interviews, I hope to gain insights into Jesus' subversive actions and teachings and what lessons we can draw from Jesus' radical empathy for the marginalized.

Richard, how does Jesus' choice to consistently stand with the underclass and marginalized provide a fresh angle on how to view power, security systems, and societal norms? Essentially, how does this perspective shake up the conventional thinking of his time?

The only way that you understand what's wrong with power is if you're powerless. The only way you understand what's wrong with security systems is if you're temporarily outside of it and insecure. What Jesus did was always take the side of the victim. The excluded one, the outsider and read reality from their side, which is to understand the real nature of the system.

The outsider, or the outcast in every system of this world, holds the secret to really understand what that system is about. That comes as a surprise to most people. That when you're inside and enjoying the fruits of any institution or any system, you don't see its idolatries and its perks and privileges, because they're supporting you, they're sustaining you, you're enjoying them, and I would be too. The one who's excluded from that system always knows that the system is other than what it says itself to be. Jesus invariably stands with the outsider, with the rejected one, and it's there that you learn compassion. It's there that you learn patience, sympathy for failure, for woundedness, for what doesn't work.

When you're always on the side of the winner, when you're always on the side of those who are succeeding inside of the system, you never really learn compassion or sympathy or patience or understanding. Someone said that a good way to understand is to stand under. And I think it's the only way to understand. To stand underneath, not on the top. And that's where Jesus consistently stands. And in that, again, he's a quite unexpected leader because he never identifies with the leadership. He always identifies with the the excluded followers.

Allen, how do you reconcile the idea that Jesus socialized with people, even in settings that some might consider objectionable, with his role as a religious figure? What are some theological interpretations of Jesus' interactions in such gatherings?

The personal engagement of Jesus with people, in some way or another, was a very important part of his ministry. He did socialize with people. And we have tradition that tries to come to terms with this. In other words, people knew that Jesus partied with people. And even today, to say it in those terms, some may find objectionable. I don't mean any disrespect. But if we talk about somebody who went to a place where people gathered together, there's a great deal of conviviality. Maybe there were some alcoholic beverages consumed. People were having a good time. Most people call it a party.

For theological reasons, we may want to call it something else, but that's what most people would call it. And Jesus frequented gatherings like that. So, that's out there. Well, what do you do with that? How do you explain that? Well, in the Gospels, one approach is to say that Jesus is like the physician who goes to people who are sick.

This is how Jesus responds. There's a question. Why do you hang out with these people? Why do you party with these people? Why do you do that? Why do we always see you hanging out with these undesirables? I mean, why are you always at the bar? That kind of thing. And the response is, "Well, the doctor doesn't go to the people who are well. He goes to the people who are sick. That's one way of responding. Then we have another stream of tradition that says, "Well, I'm sent to the lost sheep of the house of Israel. The sheep that know their way home don't need a guide. I'm sent to the people who are out there who are lost. And where are they lost? They're out there. So I'm out there.

"The Wedding at Cana from The Life, Passion and Resurrection of Christ Series," 1598 by Marten de Vos. At the Wedding at Cana, when the wine ran out, Jesus responded to his mother's request by turning water into wine, performing his first public miracle. This act not only solved a practical problem but also symbolized the abundance and joy that Jesus brings to those who believe in him.

Richard, how does Jesus continual defiance of societal norms, particularly evident in his consistent breaking of established rules underscore his subversive approach to inclusivity and social order?

Probably the most practically subversive thing Jesus constantly does is he breaks all those rules. Every time he's touching a leper, he is immediately declared unclean himself, or touching a dead body. He himself cannot go in the temple for at least three weeks. He is ritually impure. If you think that's passé, we wouldn't be so stupid, think how people who worked with AIDS patients. We're immediately considered to be…well he or she's probably one of those if he works with them. We still have that same mind.

"Christ Healing the Sick at Bethesda," 1883, by Carl Heinrich Bloch. This painting portrays Jesus interacting with lepers, possibly drawing inspiration from various accounts in the Gospels where Jesus heals those afflicted with leprosy, emphasizing themes of compassion, healing, and the inclusive nature of Jesus' ministry

Jesus always goes to those on the edge and identifies with their world. His most common audio-visual aid, wherein he breaks the rules, is the meal. Luke's gospel in particular describes ten or eleven times where Jesus sits down to eat with other people. Every time Jesus sits down to eat, he either eats the wrong food, invites the wrong people to the meal, doesn't wash his hands, sits at the wrong place at table, lets a woman come into a men's symposium and touch him.

Jesus is always breaking the rules. Because the meal was the public forum in which social order was defined. Of who was in, who was out, who was upper class, who was lower class. You think we don't do that? We still do. We know who eats certain kinds of foods, and we make fun of other kinds of foods, because those people eat those foods. It's still the same, we're just a lot more subtle about it. But you can be pretty sure which kind of food Jesus would eat and who Jesus would eat with, and who Jesus would invite to the meal.

Jesus is always expanding the meal. Putting out both ends of the table, and he uses it in his parables in Luke's gospel. Go out to the highways and the byways, the people who I invited don't want to come, and the reason they don't want to come is because all these ugly people are at the table. But go out and make them come in. Because the people I invited don't want to come to the supper.

You can almost call the New Testament the resented banquet. That God is always offering to throw a great big party. That's one of Jesus' most common images–a wedding feast, or a party, or a banquet. And no one wants to come because everybody's there. Here comes everybody, and we don't want everybody. We want church just to have us folks. This is true in every country, and I've been to a lot of places. Because most groups define themselves against another group.

Allen, how does Jesus' view of communal meals as inherently special and transcendent reflect his teachings on fellowship and gratitude?

Our experience of having a meal together is a transcendent experience. Not because Jesus had something profound to say about it. But because he teaches us that communion is transcendent. We're doing something right here and right now and it has an alimentary dimension to it. It has a dimension of conviviality to it. And we do it because we need to do it. We do it because we like to do it. There's something about us being together and enjoying together what God has given us. Amen. That is transcendent. You don't have to pronounce any magic words over that to make that special. It is special.

Allen, how does Jesus' response to criticism regarding his social behavior highlight his ability to deflect criticism back at his adversaries while also presenting himself as a relatable figure to the masses?

Jesus has another way of responding to it which is especially interesting. And this is in contrast to John the Baptist. There's a question—somebody comes to Jesus and says, "We see John's disciples. They fast. They pray. You? You're just out here hanging out all the time. What's wrong with you?" And Jesus says, "If I lie on one side I'm cursed. If I lie on the other side, I'm cursed. When John the Baptist came, he didn't drink anything. He was a teetotaler. He was a straight-up kind of guy. He was ascetic. And you said that he had some kind of mental problem. I come eating and drinking, doing what he didn't do. And now you have a problem with me. What do you want?"

In this kind of response to this criticism, there are two observations. One is that this particular response turns the criticism at the discursive level back on the adversaries. And Jesus had a reputation for being especially good at doing that. But at the critical level, just as a historical

"St. John the Baptist," painted in 1630 by Jacob Jordaens. This painting portrays John the Baptist, a central figure in the New Testament who baptized Jesus in the Jordan River, as described in the Gospel of Matthew (Chapter 3), symbolizing repentance, preparation, and the heralding of the Messiah.

observation, you have three distinct answers to one question. So the question was important. The question was, how come this guy did so much hanging out? And that was an issue. That was something that required some PR attention. It required some spin control in early Christian traditions. At another level, I think people see that and they see somebody who was a man of the people. And for the people, that has a lot of appeal.

Richard, How do you interpret the unique aspect of Hebrew scriptures, which consistently favor the marginalized and critique the powerful, and how does Jesus embody this paradigm, challenging established religion and elevating the outsider?

The Hebrew people are the only people who kept in their sacred texts, passage after passage telling them they're no good, they're phonies, they're hypocrites, they don't believe a word they say. Especially in the Prophets. And we still read these passages from Isaiah or Jeremiah and we say, "Thanks be to God." And we've just been reamed out by the word of God. The Hebrew people kept these and from this came the capacity for critical thinking, for self-criticism. When religion does not have the capacity for self-criticism, it is always idolatrous, it is always self-serving. It's not pointing to God, it's usually pointing to itself.

How the Hebrew scriptures differ from most of the sacred scriptures of the world is what Jesus finally personified. The Jewish people were not the establishment in Egypt, they were the slaves. And Moses told them this before they went into the Promised Land, when you get to the top don't forget what it's like to be on the bottom. You'll still see this in many Jewish people to this day. This bias toward the bottom. This empathy for the victim. Every significant story in the Hebrew scriptures always prefers the barren woman, the son left out in the field, the forgotten son, the rejected daughter, the sinner. It's always the person on the bottom who has it, and the person on the top who's wrong.

Once you hear this, you say, how did I never see that? That is unlike any other major literature in the world. It is absolutely unique. And it has affected the Western psyche, or those who've imbibed the scriptural mind, much more than we realize. The ultimate irony is when Christianity ends up becoming an establishment religion while worshiping the victim. We're the only religion in the world that worships the outsider, that worships the rejected one, that worships the victim. Jesus is not a natural God figure. If you were going to create a religion, you would not have thought of a naked, bleeding loser outside the city, rejected by the establishments of church and state, high priest and emperor.

Both declare he's the problem, he has to go, he's no good. And we come along, and we declare this loser the lord of history. That turned history around forever. I don't believe more than

Hear the word of the Lord,
you rulers of Sodom;
listen to the instruction of our God,
you people of Gomorrah!
'The multitude of your sacrifices—
what are they to me?' says the Lord.
'I have more than enough of burnt offerings,
of rams and the fat of fattened animals;
I have no pleasure
in the blood of bulls and lambs and goats.
When you come to appear before me,
who has asked this of you,
this trampling of my courts?
Stop bringing meaningless offerings!
Your incense is detestable to me.
New Moons, Sabbaths and convocations—
I cannot bear your worthless assemblies.
Your New Moon feasts and your appointed festivals
I hate with all my being.
They have become a burden to me;
I am weary of bearing them.
When you spread out your hands in prayer,
I hide my eyes from you;
even when you offer many prayers,
I am not listening.
Your hands are full of blood!
Wash and make yourselves clean.
Take your evil deeds out of my sight;
stop doing wrong.
Learn to do right; seek justice.
Defend the oppressed.
Take up the cause of the fatherless;
plead the case of the widow.'

Isaiah 1:10-17

10 percent of Christians ever got the point in any denomination. But there always were a few who, once you get Jesus, once you get the spirit of Jesus, once he's transformed you, you almost automatically have this empathy for the wounded one. And you have this natural mistrust of arrogance and dominative power. Because if power could have been that wrong once, that we say Jesus is the most perfect man who ever lived, and the highest authorities, high priest and emperor, say he's the problem?

So it creates, inside of us, a healthy mistrust for power. And a healthy empathy for the little guy. The excluded one, the victim, the outcast, might just be the Messiah. Might just be the one with the answer. And this is one of Jesus' most common one-liners, "The last will be first and the first will be last." He's always saying, be prepared to be surprised about who's really right. That keeps us all off-center. It keeps us all humble, which is what healthy religion is supposed to be.

Allen, How do you perceive Jesus' outreach to socially marginalized individuals within the context of Israelite tradition, and what do you believe this approach reveals about his understanding of inclusion and divine restoration?

Jesus did reach out to people who we would characterize as socially undesirable. But let's not just look at that through the lens of some romantic notion. It's clearly a strategy, an ancient strategy in Israelite tradition. One of the historical problems of Israel was that at one point Israel's political unity was disrupted. There's the Babylonian captivity, people are deported, some people leave their country and they never return. Populations of Israelites scattered all over the eastern Mediterranean. When you have these social dislocations you have destitute people in various categories who are basically written off by a society. According to Mosaic law, if you had a certain kind of handicap, you really weren't welcome in the cult. You were ritually unclean.

But there's a prophetic tradition of Israelite self-understanding that says one day when God restores the fortunes of Israel he's going to bring everybody. Not only the people who are geographically marginal, but the people who are socially marginal. So, if you are a self-respecting Israelite prophet who is standing in this tradition, then one of the things that's going to be on your agenda is to reach out to these people. Because without them, the kingdom doesn't come. You don't know that it's really here until the blind see and the lame walk and the deaf hear, the lepers are cleansed and everybody's brought into this restored commonwealth. That itself is a sign, that inclusion is itself a sign that God is at work restoring the fortunes of Israel.

So Jesus comes and he does this, and this resonates. I think it resonates with all people who've had some kind of experience of marginalization because, in effect, it's saying that God doesn't give up on anybody. And that when God is really working, somehow or another, no one's excluded from that embrace. Now, everybody may not come, but everybody's included. Everyone's invited. There are always reasons why some people don't get on the A list. There are always reasons for that. And some of those reasons are very compelling and very good.

Prophet Isaiah detail Sistine Chapel," created in 1512 by Michelangelo Buonarroti. This detail depicts the prophet Isaiah, one of the major prophets of the Old Testament, whose prophecies foretold the coming of the Messiah, including the birth of Jesus, as referenced in Isaiah 7:14 and Isaiah 9:6.

But, there's a moment where God intervenes in history where all discretion goes to the winds when it comes to compiling the A list and everybody gets on.

And when you get an A list that long, that itself is a sign that God is doing a new thing, as Isaiah put it. Isaiah is the one that says when God restores Israel's fortunes, he's going to call back all those people that were deported, he's going to bring in the lame, he's going to bring in the halt, he's going to bring in the person who's poor, the eunuch who is ritually unclean. Don't call yourself a dry tree, don't say that you're useless. Everybody's going to have a place. And the people who think that they ought to have a place, are the folks that are going to get turned away at the door. And not just the men which is so appealing to so many of the downtrodden and particularly women.

Reflections

In this section of the film, the main point being driven home is that Jesus recognizes and acts on the premise that true understanding of power comes from experiencing powerlessness. He takes the side of the "victim," as Father Rohr expresses. This perspective is echoed in Matthew 20:26-28. I find it particularly interesting how the passage frames Jesus' approach to leadership and empathy. His consistent choice to stand with the excluded and marginalized rather than aligning with the powerful offers a profound lesson in humility and compassion.

It underscores the idea that true leadership involves a deep connection with and understanding of the most vulnerable members of society. It makes me consider how often those in positions of power are

> "Whoever wants to become great among you must be your servant, and whoever wants to be first must be your slave— just as the Son of Man did not come to be served, but to serve, and to give his life as a ransom for many."
>
> (Matthew 20:26-28)

oblivious to the injustices and inequalities perpetuated by the very systems that benefit them. This perspective is not only thought-provoking but also deeply relevant to contemporary discussions about social justice and equity.

Jesus' outreach to socially undesirable individuals isn't solely an expression of compassion but also a strategic move grounded in ancient Israelite tradition. Allen's pointing out the notion that the Hebrew scriptures uniquely emphasize self-criticism and empathy for the marginalized is important for those who focus more on the New Testament, as I do, particularly the Gospels. The idea that the Torah contains extensive passages of self-rebuke and calls out hypocrisy is quite striking. That was the playbook that Jesus was operating from. It suggests that these texts are designed to encourage continuous reflection and humility among their followers, fostering a culture where questioning and self-examination are integral to faith.

This contrasts sharply with the tendency of many religious traditions to present their beliefs and practices as beyond reproach, which can lead to self-serving interpretations. This is something that seems to come up again and again in Jesus' encounters with the religious leaders of his time. It highlights how the Hebrew scriptures consistently champion the underdog—the barren woman, the forgotten son, the sinner—over the powerful and established. Jesus clearly echoes these teachings in his mission.

Father Rohr points out that this paradoxical worship of a rejected, suffering figure as the central deity of Christianity is both unique and revolutionary. It challenges the conventional association of divinity with power and success. The passage makes me think about how this orientation towards empathy for the victim and skepticism of power should fundamentally shape Christian attitudes and behaviors. Yet, ironically, even with the benefit of Jesus' clear teachings in the Gospels, Christianity has become an "establishment religion," which very often loses sight of its core message; that true wisdom and salvation may come from those on the margins. This critique serves as a powerful reminder of the importance of continuously re-evaluating how religious teachings are applied in the context of power and authority.

One of my favorite characteristics of Jesus is that he often engages with people in social settings that we might consider unconventional for a religious leader. If we fully acknowledge one type of setting that is referenced often, many would elevate that from unconventional to inappropriate. It is the image of Jesus "partying with people," as Allen described it. Or, as he would frame it in more palatable terms, Jesus often attends gatherings where festivity and perhaps even alcoholic beverages are present—a challenge to traditional perceptions of religious propriety. At the same time, this portrayal makes Jesus appear more approachable and human, emphasizing his willingness to meet people where they are rather than expecting them to come to him in a state of righteousness or piety.

The analogy of Jesus as a physician who goes to the sick, rather than waiting for the sick to come to him, is also powerful. It implies that true leadership and compassion involve actively seeking out and addressing the needs of those who are most in need of support and guidance. Moreover, the notion of being sent to the "lost sheep" and the emphasis on reaching those who are "out there" rather than those who are already on the right path highlight the radical inclusivity of Jesus' ministry that certainly made the temple cult uncomfortable. This is evident throughout the Gospels, such as in Luke 7:36-50, where Jesus dines with a Pharisee and allows a sinful woman to wash his feet, challenging societal expectations and norms.

Another less controversial but equally symbolic setting that we see Jesus and his disciples participating in is the communal meal, which Father Rohr views as inherently special and transcendent. Jesus elevates the significance of shared meals as moments of communion and connection, reflecting the divine presence in community. What is it about the meal in particular that makes it so central to his movement? It is clearly important. Father Rohr returns to this theme repeatedly in his writings and lectures.

Perhaps the act of sharing meals has a profound ability to connect people and break down social barriers because it taps into our most primal instincts and cultural practices. When we gather to cook and eat together, we engage in a ritual that transcends mere sustenance. The collaborative effort of preparing food fosters a sense of unity and shared purpose that is rare in other activities. This unity extends to the dining table, where the physical closeness and the act of sharing dishes create an environment ripe for building trust and camaraderie. Serving food to one another is an act of generosity that can dissolve social hierarchies, placing everyone on equal footing, at least for the duration of the meal.

If we get even more granular, I would speculate that this power is rooted in our evolutionary history, where early humans depended on shared meals for survival, creating strong social bonds necessary for cooperation and communal living. This connection to our past, combined with the symbolic power of food as nourishment and care, transforms shared meals into a powerful tool for fostering inclusivity and understanding. The relaxed atmosphere of a meal encourages open, meaningful conversations and cultural exchange, highlighting our shared human experiences and breaking down the barriers that divide us.

Woman, you have great faith! VI

Matthew 15:28

Much like Jesus' embrace of "Sinners" and societal outcasts we just explored, I am interested in the ways in which his trust in and affirmation of women's faith in particular, especially those deemed outsiders by Jewish norms, shaped the early movement. While men were more commonly accepted as leaders and teachers, Jesus' intentional inclusion of women in key roles served as a profound challenge to the deeply ingrained patriarchal traditions of the time. How did this radical approach redefine the social and spiritual landscape?

Reflecting on the broader role women may have played in sustaining and advancing Jesus' ministry, what does this suggest about Jesus' role, not only as a spiritual leader but also as a pragmatic strategist who recognized the essential role of inclusivity in ensuring the success and longevity of his mission? Richard has written and spoken about one surprising way women contributed to sustaining the movement that I had never considered and just might surprise you too.

I've often wondered why Jesus did not include women among his disciples. Women brought a profound spiritual strength that fueled the movement, and while their contributions may have differed, they were likely just as crucial. Given Jesus' teachings, this seems entirely logical. So why has their involvement been so frequently overlooked or minimized?

In this section of the film I want to better understand how Jesus' intentional empowerment of women, especially those marginalized, subverted societal norms and was essential to the enduring influence of the early Christian movement.

"The Wedding at Cana (detail from the Scrovegni Chapel frescoes)," created in 1305 by Giotto di Bondone. In this detail, a group of women stands behind Jesus, possibly reflecting the presence of Mary, the mother of Jesus, and other female attendees at the wedding feast, symbolizing their witness to Jesus' miracle and their role in his ministry, as portrayed in the Gospel of John, Chapter 2.

Allen, how do you assess the significance of the involvement of women in Jesus' ministry, given the subordinate role they held within first-century Palestinian society? Furthermore, how do we ascertain the extent of their actual involvement, considering the historical context and available evidence?

I don't know how unusual it is that Jesus would actually have women with him, or associated with him. Maybe the manner of association is unusual. That they were somehow involved integrally with what he was doing. I don't think that this means that the patriarchal norms of first-century Palestine were obliterated in the ministry of Jesus. I don't think that's historically possible. I think that would have been absolutely incoherent to everybody at the time.

But women were involved and the traditions are very clear about it. Modern New Testament scholarship has these criteria for discerning historical verisimilitude—what's most historically likely. One of those criteria is called the "criterion of embarrassment", and it works like this: If you find a tradition that says something that a lot of people didn't want to say, or didn't want to be said, but it survives, the chance is pretty good that's historical. Because if people could have been able to exercise some kind of spin control over that and suppress it, they would have done so.

Richard, considering the evidence from scripture that indicates the involvement of women in the movement surrounding Jesus, why do you think all of the disciples mentioned were men?

I think the first socio-cultural reason is because in his time, they would have been the only ones who would have been taken seriously as leaders of anything. They were the only ones who were accepted as teachers or as credible witnesses. It was a Jewish patriarchal world and society. A woman would not have been allowed to lead anything. And it seems that Jesus did want to communicate a message. He wanted to create multipliers, if you will. In that sense, he showed a certain practical genius.

But I guess I'd add I think he chose men and taught men to do it in a different way. A way of living without power. Like when he sends them out, two by two. All the teaching is teaching of vulnerability and powerlessness. He's almost setting them up to be rejected and to fail. It's their initiation right, if you will. And he's telling them, okay, how are you going to deal with

Calling the Twelve to him, he began to send them out two by two and gave them authority over impure spirits. These were his instructions: "Take nothing for the journey except a staff—no bread, no bag, no money in your belts." Mark 6:7-8

"Christ in the House of Martha and Mary," painted in 1655 by Johannes Vermeer. This painting depicts the biblical scene from the Gospel of Luke (Chapter 10, verses 38-42), where Jesus visits the home of Martha and Mary, showcasing the contrast between Martha's busyness with household chores and Mary's attentive listening to Jesus' teachings, inviting reflection on the balance between action and contemplation in the Christian life.

that? How are you going to deal with being at the bottom of the pile instead of the top? Jesus didn't need to teach that to women.

Richard, how do you interpret the historical positioning of women in a subordinate role within society and its impact on their spiritual development? And how would you describe the role of women in the Gospels, particularly regarding Jesus' interactions with them and their faith?

"The Feast in the House of Simon the Pharisee," painted between 1618-1620 by Peter Paul Rubens. This painting portrays the biblical event described in the Gospel of Luke (Chapter 7, verses 36-50), where a sinful woman anoints Jesus' feet with perfume and washes them with her tears during a meal at the house of Simon the Pharisee, illustrating themes of forgiveness, repentance, and the transformative power of grace.

Women have always been in the one down position in culture. Now that gave them a head start in terms of spirituality. You see, whenever you're in the one down position, the excluded one, you have a head start symbolically in understanding wisdom. We see that Jesus had no trouble relating to women as authority figures. When you read the Gospels, you see that women actually did play a fairly significant role. It's not often that we hear that.

Jesus consistently trusts women and recognizes that they have so much faith. He will again and again say, "Never have I found such faith. Go in peace." he doesn't tell them to come back and join the Jewish religion in Jerusalem. He says, "Go in peace, go on the path you're on. Your faith has made you whole." That's really a quite dangerous talk. That shows how much he trusted these women's journey. And many of them were not Jewish women. They were pagans by Jewish standards. And he still told them, "Go your way, your faith has made you whole." That is subversive.

Allen, could you provide an example of a pivotal initiative within the movement that women may have led, but hasn't received adequate attention in terms of its significance or impact? Additionally, can you delve into the reasons why it might have been overlooked?

The Gospel of Luke is very clear at one point. It says that Jesus was traveling with these women, and that they were supporting him. So there's a very strong memory of women being involved in the movement, as it were, and bankrolling it, to some extent. I think everybody knows this. Maybe

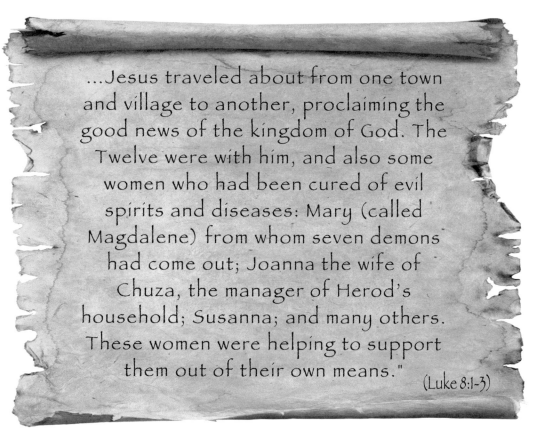

...Jesus traveled about from one town and village to another, proclaiming the good news of the kingdom of God. The Twelve were with him, and also some women who had been cured of evil spirits and diseases: Mary (called Magdalene) from whom seven demons had come out; Joanna the wife of Chuza, the manager of Herod's household; Susanna; and many others. These women were helping to support them out of their own means." (Luke 8:1-3)

not everybody is all choked up about it, but everybody knows it.

But as we've discussed, certain social habits that Jesus had were embarrassing, I think, to later people. To later Christians. Socializing with socially undesirable people. Socializing, partying. This is a big part of Jesus' public profile. For some people, this is problematic. Association with women, and women being involved in what he was doing. People who could be involved and were disposed to be involved were invited to be involved. And what they were or where they came from wasn't as important as their willingness to be involved. And when you couple that with an ideology that says that when whatever it is is working right, everybody has a place in it. There's a fit there. There's a very, very tight and compelling fit there that brought women in, that brought other people in. And they came in, they found a place and they stayed.

Richard, in what way would you say that Jesus valued women in the movement? Could you provide an example that may not have been explicitly evident in scripture or perhaps hasn't received acknowledgment for various reasons?

In terms of Jesus' relationship to women, many modern feminists admit that he's a man out of due time. He is not a typical man of his age or religion. He treats women consistently with dignity, with respect. He's invariably saying to women, come up, trust yourself. You can read the whole gospel that way.

"The Resurrection of Christ (detail from the Scrovegni Chapel frescoes)," painted in 1305 by Giotto di Bondone. This detail highlights Mary Magdalene witnessing the resurrected Jesus Christ, emphasizing her significant role as the first to encounter the risen Lord, as recounted in the Gospel of John (Chapter 20, verses 11-18), symbolizing her deep devotion and the profound encounter with divine grace.

Probably the most striking example of that is this figure, Mary Magdalene. Now, I know we Christians all assume that she was a prostitute, it really never says that. Of course, there are different Marys mentioned. But it mentions a woman who had seven demons. We just assume, of course, that the demon was lust. It never says that at all. But the interesting thing about this woman is that she is the first one that Jesus appears to after the resurrection. Which clearly means she had some significant meaning in his life. She believes, and she becomes the messenger to the messengers. She has to convince the twelve apostles that Jesus has risen. We now have evidence in the first thousand years of Christianity, she was recognized as an apostle, even the first of the apostles, because she believed in the resurrection, first of all, before they did.

The angel said to the women, "Do not be afraid, for I know that you are looking for Jesus, who was crucified. He is not here; he has risen, just as he said. Come and see the place where he lay. Then go quickly and tell his disciples: 'He has risen from the dead and is going ahead of you into Galilee. There you will see him.' Now I have told you."
So the women hurried away from the tomb, afraid yet filled with joy, and ran to tell his disciples.
Suddenly Jesus met them. "Greetings," he said. They came to him, clasped his feet and worshiped him. Then Jesus said to them, "Do not be afraid. Go and tell my brothers to go to Galilee; there they will see me."

Matthew 28:5-10

Richard, How do you think the historical and societal perceptions of gender roles have influenced our understanding of spiritual figures, particularly Jesus?

If God had come into the world in the body of a woman and been patient and nurturing and sensitive and social, we would have said, yeah, business as usual. But God came into the world in the body of a man, and did it unlike men do it. He was not a typical male, certainly not a macho male in any sense. He consistently refused every attempt at dominative power over anything or anybody. I don't think human history and human consciousness were ready for that. I wouldn't blame anybody. I think that the masculine consciousness seemed to have happened first in civilization. We needed order, structure, boundaries, identity, clarity, if you will. That's the masculine mind.

But if you look at the teaching of Jesus, he's not concerned about those things. He's more into the world of paradox, mystery, subtlety, forgiving of enemies, understanding the other side. That's more feminine energy. I don't think history was ready for Jesus and that paradox. But what's happening right now in human history is that perhaps for the first time on a major level, many people seem ready to understand how utterly revolutionary the mind of Jesus was and the teaching of Jesus was.

We've come very much from the side of either-or, right or wrong, good or bad, dualistic thinking where you can deal with clarity and order. But fill that with subtlety and compassion? That's wisdom. Every religion uses that word wisdom for that wonderful synthesis or integration between order and compassion. Having the rules and breaking the rules. And to know how to do that. To know how to have the rules, but know when the rules have to be broken. That's spiritual genius. And Jesus personifies it to an enormous degree.

Reflections

What I found particularly interesting in this section of the film was the uncovering of the nuanced approach Jesus took in integrating women into his ministry, which appears both strategic and radical for his time. While the patriarchal norms of first-century Palestine were firmly established, Jesus' inclusion of women in significant roles within his ministry subtly challenged these norms. One of the most surprising examples of this was Father Rohr clearly pointing out that women were helping to finance the Jesus movement out of their own pockets, as described in the Gospel of Luke. These contributions have often been under-appreciated or overlooked altogether.

When we look at these critical, timely, and consistent contributions from women, we may want to minimize their impact, ignore them, or worse, deny that they happened at all. Allen raises the point that this becomes more difficult based on the principle of the "criterion of embarrassment," which many modern New Testament scholars use to assert the historical authenticity of these traditions. This method suggests that since these stories survived despite cultural resistance, they are likely rooted in historical truth. This approach allows us to see Jesus not only as a spiritual leader but also as a pragmatic strategist who recognized the importance of inclusivity for the effectiveness and sustainability of his mission.

Accepting that women had such a critical role, I was very interested in understanding why Jesus did not have any among his disciples. Father Rohr explains that the selection of male disciples can be understood within the socio-cultural context of the time, where men were taken more seriously as leaders. They were the only ones who were accepted as teachers. But he goes on to say that by choosing men and teaching them to embrace vulnerability and powerlessness, Jesus was creating leaders who understood the value of humility and service, in contrast to the prevailing norms of dominance and authority. Women, who were already accustomed to being marginalized, had an intrinsic understanding of these values.

Jesus' trust in and affirmation of women's faith and spiritual journeys, even those who were considered outsiders by Jewish standards, underscores a profound message of universal acceptance and the potential for spiritual wisdom in unexpected places. This radical inclusivity was revolutionary for his time and aligns with modern feminist ideals. The example of Mary Magdalene, often misunderstood and mischaracterized, underscores the significance of women's roles in early Christianity. As Richard Rohr says, she wasn't just considered an apostle in the early Christian tradition but the first of the apostles. Her role as the first witness to the resurrection and her task of convincing the apostles highlight her pivotal position in the Christian narrative.

As Father Rohr points out, the revolutionary nature of Jesus' teachings, which transcended traditional masculine norms, was ahead of its time. This can be observed in qualities he exhibited typically associated with women—such as patience, nurturing, sensitivity, and a refusal to exert dominative power—despite being a man. This juxtaposition of Jesus' identity as a male with his

"The Penitent Magdalene," 1576, El Greco. This scene illustrates the power of forgiveness and redemption in Jesus' ministry, highlighting the theme of repentance and the profound change that comes from accepting Jesus' grace and mercy as described in Luke 7:37-38.

rejection of traditional masculine roles and his embrace of qualities often undervalued in men suggests a deliberate subversion of societal expectations and norms, presenting a revolutionary model of leadership and humanity. This concept challenges the deeply ingrained binary thinking of "masculine" and "feminine" traits, encouraging a more integrated and holistic approach to understanding human potential and divinity.

VII "Don't be afraid..."

As I described in the introduction, my early experiences with representations of the divine in European churches and cathedrals left a lasting impression. The dark, cold, and intimidating paintings and icons that I internalized conveyed a sense of foreboding. This feeling also seeped into the sermons I listened to for years as I grew older, though not as overtly.

For centuries, humanity has grappled with a pervasive fear of God. This fear is evident across cultures and history, often manifesting in extreme rituals and sacrifices intended to appease a seemingly wrathful deity. Why did people historically perceive God as someone to be feared? What circumstances led to such widespread practices, and what were people hoping to achieve through these acts of devotion that were happening in Jesus' time?

The contrast between what appears to be a more vengeful God of the Old Testament and a loving God of the New Testament seems to be a common theme. This is an area that I have a lot of questions about. Why is there such a stark difference between these depictions? The New Testament alludes to this fear often – for example, angels often begin interactions with "Do not be afraid." What does this repeated assurance suggest about people's perceptions of divine beings at that time? How did Jesus address this dynamic in his teachings? Is the distinction between the vengeful Old Testament God and the loving New Testament God a fair one, or is there more complexity to this issue? How did Jesus present both God's mercy and judgment in a way that resonated with his followers?

In the Gospels, we see Jesus referring to God as "Father" and speaking of God's care for everyone. I am interested in understanding what anxieties or doubts Jesus addresses with this message. How does his portrayal of a loving, caring God contrast with the existing beliefs and fears of the people around him, and what impact does this have on his audience's understanding of their relationship with God?

Intriguingly, Jesus' teachings also convey a sense of urgency. He speaks of God actively working in the world and the need for an immediate response. I am interested in what causes this sense of urgency in Jesus' message. Why does he emphasize the need for a prompt reaction to God's call, and how does this urgency affect the way people respond to his teachings and the spread of his message?

"HELL," painted in 1505 by Hieronymus Bosch. In this painting Bosch creates a vivid and surreal depiction of the torments of hell, which could be interpreted as a cautionary visual representation of biblical concepts of sin, judgment, and the consequences of moral wrongdoing. He often portrays surreal and nightmarish scenes of torment and punishment, reflecting his fascination with themes of sin, morality, and the afterlife.

Richard, how might the transition in cultural perceptions of divinity, from fear and apprehension to a message of fearlessness and love, inform our understanding of Jesus' teachings?

We know now from cultural historical study that up to the time of Abraham, human sacrifice was found on every continent, if you go back far enough. That human beings felt God was basically dangerous, toxic, someone to be afraid of. And for some strange reason the human mind felt if we would kill our best and our brightest that this might placate this angry God.

Around the time of Abraham, and it happened in many places in the world, we see that culture moved to animal sacrifice. By the time Jesus comes, we know that 90 percent of the economy of the city of Jerusalem had to do with the buying and selling of animals, the penning of animals, the butchering of animals by priests, and the hauling of the animals out by the tens of thousands after every feast day.

And that's why every theophany, every divine apparition in the whole Bible is preceded or begins with the identical same phrase. It always starts with the angel or the messenger or the God figure saying, "Do not be afraid." They had to begin with "do not be afraid" because normally when God broke into history you had every reason to be afraid. God always wanted your blood.

"Scenes from the Life of Joachim (detail from the Scrovegni Chapel frescoes)," painted in 1305 by Giotto di Bondone.

What we have on the cross is the turnaround of all historic religion. And we've seen this cross so often as Christians we don't get its historical, secular meaning. Suddenly on the cross, we have God spilling blood to get to us. And in that saying, my God, it's a safe world. God is not toxic. God is not dangerous. God is not out after you. God is not cruel and punishing and blaming and vengeful. In the risen Christ you have a figure who refuses to blame anybody. And he identifies forgiveness with his very breath. Now, anybody would be attracted by such a figure. Just a quintessentially rich and deep and profound human being. I think if you can allow yourself to be drawn by his humanity, God will take care of it from there.

Allen, how does the perception of God's nature and character evolve between the Old and New Testaments, and how might this evolution challenge traditional understandings?

Well, the traditional contrast between the wrathful jealous God of the Old Testament and the God of love in the New Testament is greatly overdrawn. And Jewish theologians have pointed this out. Moses told us that God is slow to anger and plenteous in mercy. And the historical project, if you will, of Israel would have been impossible without a great deal of forbearance on God's part. And this is how Israel understands itself—as God cutting Israel a break dramatically, not because of any merit that Israel has, but because of God's mercy. God does things simply because God is good.

And this isn't such a compelling reason, but this is good enough for God. There would be no hope for a restoration of Israel if God didn't exercise a certain amount of forbearance. Israel was judged for falling short of God's ordinances. Many prophetic traditions of Israel say that God won't always be angry. The guy's incapable of holding a grudge. And that one day God will

"The Creation of the Sun, the Moon and the Stars (detail from the Sistine Chapel Frescoes)," painted in 1511 by Michelangelo Buonarroti. This detail depicts the moment from the book of Genesis (Chapter 1, verses 14-19) where God creates the celestial bodies, illustrating divine creation and the unfolding of the universe according to biblical narrative.

restore Israel's fortunes. This wrathful angry God is not without foundation in the Bible. But these two sides of God, the God of anger and the God of forbearance and mercy, are cheek by jowl.

So it's a problem of theology to reconcile them. And part of the problem is the intellectual baggage that we bring to it. Analysis takes apart complex things. But truth be told, analysis really doesn't like complexity. So we don't like complex people. And so even though most people are complex, we kind of flatten them out. They're type A, type B. The God of Israel is complex and some of those facets are highlighted in the ministry of Jesus.

Jesus does talk quite a bit about those more unsavory sides too, such as judgment, that we don't like to talk about. He talked a lot about hell. The definition of hell and heaven, even in the words of Jesus, is a challenge of theological interpretation. But clearly when he talked about the kingdom, he was talking about an experience that we have in the world, in history. Otherwise, what's the point? You don't have to organize people for any kind of project that's going to take place on the other side of history. No, his understanding was that human beings participate in this. And this too is a feature of ancient Israelite conviction.

That God wants to dwell in the midst of the people and work out a project in history with people. That God doesn't want to go it alone. Now you would think that with all the trouble it causes God to have partners, especially given his qualifications, that he would go it alone. But he doesn't. And Israel is a part of that process.

And God is insistent that the process go forward. So, God draws people to himself. And this drawing is part of the attraction of Jesus' ministry. Not so much that Jesus is charismatic in some kind of Bavarian sense that made women faint. But that in him, God was making an appeal to people. They had a lot of reasons not to come. But they had an invitation from God. So with all the reasons that they had not to come, and all the reasons that other people gave them not to come, God was giving them a very compelling reason to come.

Richard, how does the depiction of the risen Christ as one who places no blame challenge traditional views of divine judgment and retribution? And what does this portrayal suggest about the evolving understanding of God's nature throughout human history?

Finally, we see in the risen Christ one who blames nobody. We've been afraid of God for all of human history. And suddenly we have in the risen Christ, and it takes the whole Bible to get us there - two steps forward and three steps backward. You can almost say that the Bible is edging toward a nonviolent God.

Of course, it's not that God was ever violent. It's that we were. And we projected onto God what we were comfortable with. We made God into our own image. As some have said, God created us in God's image, and we returned the compliment. We largely made God into what we wanted God to be. And because we were a violent people, a hateful people, an aggressive people, we basically made God into the same.

But the good news is that at the end of the Bible is a totally nonblaming, nonaccusing, nonviolent God. Jesus, after the crucifixion, betrayal, abandonment of his inner circle doesn't even mention it. In fact, to the one who, who was supposedly the first pope, St. Peter denied him three times, all he does is give him three chances to say, I love you. I love you. Imagine how it must have dawned on Peter's mind what had just happened. He took away my shame. That is what the biblical God is finally doing. Always taking away this human shame that begins already in Genesis.

Really, it's the first thing we hear about these human people. They're afraid that they're naked. They want to cover themselves. And the first words of God is, "Who told you you were naked?" And it takes the rest of the Bible for God to take away our shame about being naked human beings. So the Christian religion is not presenting God as an idea, but God as a person. And truth is not a concept that you can argue about. Christian truth, at its best, is a person.

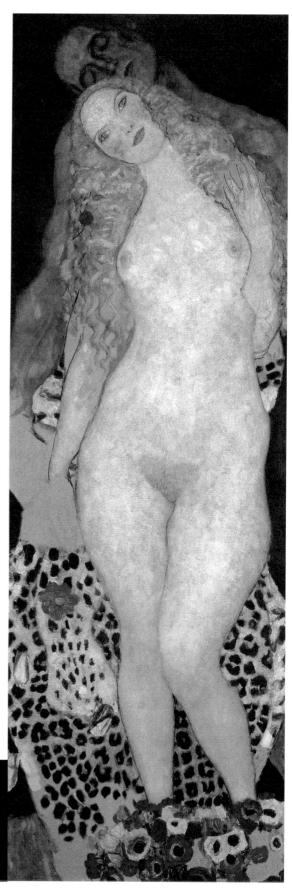

"Adam and Eve," painted in 1917 by Gustav Klimt. This painting depicts the biblical figures of Adam and Eve, reflecting the narrative from the Book of Genesis (Chapter 2-3), symbolizing the origins of humanity, the temptation, and the fall from grace, which could be interpreted as a commentary on human nature and the human condition.

Allen, how did Jesus convey the concept of God's care and involvement through the imagery of God as a father, and what reassurance did this offer to those who doubted or felt unworthy of God's love?

Jesus challenged his audience to believe that God was going to take care of them. That God was already taking care of them. That God was already involved. That God was already concerned. In the very nomenclature of God that he used referring to God as a father. Talking about the love of God the way we talk about the relationship between parents and children to assure people who had real doubts about the love and care of God. And had really good reasons to doubt the love and care of God. And how worthy they might be or deserving they might be of that love and care. That, that was not a problem. That was not the issue. That God's love and care was very real. And that their anxiety, their anguish, their concerns that constitute life in the world, are not just misunderstandings.

You're in pain, that pain is real. You have shame, that shame is real. You have anxiety because you don't know where your next meal is coming from, that's real. And because it's real, God is doing something about that, even if you don't believe it. And if you look around, there are indications that God is doing something about that.

So in those moments when we have difficulty believing in the goodness of God and life being as it is, there are many. We can see that goodness refracted through the lens of the words of Jesus. That's why those words are compelling for us.

Richard, how did the embodiment of God in a relatable form make God more tangible and relatable to humanity?

God had to come in an attractive form, a believable form, a warm and trustful form that made God touchable, believable, credible, and even "imitatable." You don't know how to be a certain way until you see another person do it. If you're a loving person today, I can say with almost total certitude it's because you've met some loving people along the way and you watched them. You

> The Word became flesh and made his dwelling among us. We have seen his glory, the glory of the one and only Son, who came from the Father, full of grace and truth.
>
> (John 1:14)

"The Visit of the Queen of Sheba to King Solomon," painted in 1890 by Edward Poynter. This painting depicts the biblical account from the First Book of Kings (Chapter 10), where the Queen of Sheba visits King Solomon, symbolizing wisdom, wealth, and the exchange of knowledge,

watched how they do it. How do you do love? If you're a patient person, I'll bet you had a patient mother or a patient father.

We're very mimetic. We rub off on one another. And so God, it seems, could not be content to be an idea, or a concept, or a theory, or a theology, which is what we've made God into. Something we can argue about and be right about and have God as our private possession in our pocket. But instead, God became "flesh," as John says.

Allen, earlier we discussed Jesus' use of nature as metaphor in his teachings. Can you elaborate on how he employed nature to alleviate fear, as repeatedly encouraged by the angels?

There are a lot of disputes about what sayings are attributed to Jesus. But there's one image in the tradition that draws an analogy between the goodness of God and the abundance of nature. The indiscriminate bounty of nature. That the sun shines on the just and the unjust. The rain falls on the just and the unjust. God has a capacity to be good to everybody. There's a kind of indiscriminate goodness about God. He's good for no reason to everybody.

Jesus says look at the lilies of the field. Look at the beautiful colors and how they're so beautifully arrayed. And he talks about King Solomon and his resplendent kingdom. He said Solomon never had a wardrobe like these. Look at these flowers. He never looked so good with all of his cash. He never had a wardrobe that equaled this. Now, what's going to happen to these flowers? After the season, you're going to throw them in the oven, they're going to dry up and die. He says, you don't have to worry about what you're going to wear. God will take care of that. You don't have to worry about what you're going to eat. You see these birds, they're flying around here. Who feeds them? God feeds them. And you've got to believe that you're worth more than a bunch of birds. God is very good. He's going to take care of you too. So don't worry about it.

Jesus' message often carried a sense of urgency. Why was this, and can you provide a clear example from the Gospels?

There was an urgency because God was doing something in people's lives in history. That means it has a temporal and a spatial dimension. It's happening here and now. It's not something that you can just wait for, like you're waiting for a bus. "Well, if I miss this one, another one will come along in about five minutes." No. God is doing something right now. It's not going to come along in another ten minutes. It didn't come along ten minutes ago. It's happening right now. And if you're going to get with this program, you gotta get with it right now.

Now, that's quite a challenge in all ages, because people always have other things that they're doing. And so we have stories about Jesus encountering these people and saying, "Well, look, you know, yeah, I'd like to get with this project. It's very compelling. But you see my father's just passed away and I, you know, I've got to tend to the funeral." And Jesus says "Forget your father. He's dead." That's the last act of filial piety in any traditional society. "Forget him." he says. "Let the dead bury the dead."

People marshal various excuses for why they can't get with the program, and he's got an answer for all of these. And those answers are all very unflattering, unsavory, and hard. The project demands attention immediately. God hasn't postponed it, and neither can any of the other principles, as it were.

> And when he got into the boat, his disciples followed him. And behold, there arose a great storm on the sea, so that the boat was being swamped by the waves; but he was asleep. And they went and woke him, saying, 'Save us, Lord; we are perishing.' And he said to them, 'Why are you afraid, O you of little faith?'
>
> Matthew 8:23-26

"Christ In The Storm On The Sea Of Galilee," painted in 1633 by Rembrandt van Rijn. This painting depicts the biblical scene from the Gospel of Mark (Chapter 4, verses 35-41) where Jesus calms a storm while crossing the Sea of Galilee with his disciples, symbolizing Jesus' divine power over nature and his ability to bring peace and safety to his followers amidst turmoil.

Reflections

One of the things I am most interested in understanding is the contrast between the desperate way people flock to Jesus and the more fear-based obedience that I encounter in the portrayal of a wrathful God in the Old Testament. Along those lines, Father Rohr points out that this is in part why one of the most mentioned phrases in the Bible is "Do not be afraid." As he describes, it underscores the pervasive fear humans have towards God and highlights the gradual transformation in humanity's understanding of him. I find the role of angels in this dynamic particularly interesting.

The angels are not just messengers but heralds of a new relationship between God and humanity—one not based on fear and appeasement but on reassurance and love. By consistently urging people not to be afraid, angels symbolize the evolving nature of divine-human interaction, setting the stage for the ultimate revelation of God's true nature through Jesus. Jesus' life and sacrifice further this message, portraying God not as vengeful but as compassionate and loving, thereby completing the transformation that the angels' words had begun to initiate.

What's interesting here is the idea that the Bible progressively reveals a God who is not violent, contrary to human projections. As Father Rohr says, "God made us in his image, and we returned the favor." This encapsulates the idea that human perceptions have shaped our understanding of God, but the ultimate revelation in the Bible is of a God who is entirely different from our flawed, violent selves. This understanding calls for a shift from viewing God through the lens of human aggression to seeing God as a being who fundamentally seeks to remove shame and promote peace.

Allen further challenges the common belief that the God of the Old Testament is wrathful while the God of the New Testament is loving. As someone who focuses on the Gospels for this film, Allen drives home the point that both anger and mercy are present in God's nature throughout the Bible. This is essential for understanding Israel's theology, which views itself as being continually shown mercy by God, despite its shortcomings. God's character is complex and can't be neatly categorized. God's wrath and mercy coexist, showing a divine nature that is multifaceted. God's actions are driven by inherent goodness, not by human merit.

Jesus' ministry highlights this duality, talking about both judgment and mercy. His teachings on hell and heaven illustrate the challenge of interpreting theological concepts, showing that God's nature and intentions are intricate. The idea that God seeks a relationship with humanity, drawing people to him through Jesus, reflects a deep desire for a divine connection.

Allen also highlights Jesus' message that God's care and involvement in human lives are constant and assured, using the metaphor of a parent-child relationship to illustrate this divine love. This message is particularly significant for people who have valid reasons to doubt God's love and care due to their real-life anxieties and struggles. Allen powerfully frames it: "their anxiety, their anguish, their concerns that constitute life in the world, are not just misunderstandings. You're in pain, that pain is real. You have shame, that shame is real. You have anxiety because you don't know where your next meal is coming from, that's real."

What stands out is Jesus' acknowledgment of human suffering and doubt, affirming that these feelings are valid and not mere misunderstandings. Jesus assures his audience that despite their pain, shame, and anxiety, God's love and care are unwavering and active. Jesus' teachings encourage believers to trust in God's care even when circumstances seem bleak. By likening God's love to that of a parent, Jesus makes the divine relationship more relatable and reassuring.

As earlier stated, much of my focus is unearthing the human Jesus, who in many ways becomes overshadowed when viewed through the lens of organized religion. Father Rohr comments on how God needed to become tangible and relatable, appearing in a form that humans could see, touch, and imitate. People learn by watching others, and if God stayed an abstract concept, God would remain distant and debatable—something to argue about but not experience personally.

What's intriguing is the emphasis on God becoming flesh, as described in the Gospel of John. This makes God's nature understandable and approachable. By becoming a human, God moves beyond being just an idea to being a living example of how to live. Again, God's incarnation as Jesus bridges the gap between the divine and human, making divine qualities accessible and imitable. This is echoed in what I already discussed in the Great Commandment—loving your neighbor as a bridge to loving God.

Allen points out that "Don't be afraid" is important, but equally important is don't delay. Jesus' encounters with individuals who offer excuses for delaying their participation underscore the uncompromising nature of this call. What stands out to me is the intense urgency he places on responding to God's call without delay. His responses to those who hesitate illustrate the critical importance of seizing the moment to participate in God's work. As Allen describes, it's not like you're waiting for a bus; the opportunity may not come around again.

What was most jolting was the response he gave to the man whose father had just passed away. To a casual bystander, "Let the dead bury the dead" sounds pretty harsh, particularly when it is your own family. Jesus' stark responses to excuses reveal that the demands of the divine project surpass traditional social and familial obligations, reflecting a radical shift in values. He urges believers to recognize the paramount importance of aligning with God's active presence in their lives immediately, highlighting the transient nature of human life and the need to act decisively in response to God's ongoing work in the world.

VIII

We have found this man subverting our nation...

Luke 23:2

This section of *Portrait of a Radical* is the part of the Jesus Movement that captures my attention most profoundly. Jesus walks into a highly charged time in Palestine with a very provocative and dangerous message. Words like respect and admiration feel too weak to convey how I feel about his willingness to lay everything on the line from day one—a level of faith and courage on an epic scale.

Jesus must have known his time to act would not be open-ended. In fact, at approximately the midpoint of the movement, in the Gospel of Mark 8:31, Jesus begins to teach his disciples about his impending suffering, saying, "He then began to teach them that the Son of Man must suffer many things and be rejected by the elders, the chief priests and the teachers of the law, and that he must be killed...." From that point on, he doesn't tone down his message; he amplifies it.

I want to understand the historical context in which Jesus lives. How do the political and social conditions of first-century Palestine shape his ministry? Palestine is divided into regions with different rulers, and there is significant tension between these authorities and the people. What impact does this have on Jesus and his teachings?

I'm intrigued by how Roman imperialism and the economic disparity of the time influence his message. Jesus often speaks out against the established religious norms, and I want to know more about why his teachings seem to undermine the traditional views he is exposed to. How do the oppressive Roman rule and the corruption within the religious authorities contribute to this?

I also want to understand Jesus' actions, like overturning the money changers' tables in the temple. Why is this event so significant, and how does it directly challenge the religious leaders of his time and really put the wheels in motion for his execution? I am curious about how his simple teachings, such as loving God and neighbor, threaten the complex legalistic system maintained by the scribes and Pharisees.

Moreover, I am intrigued by Jesus' claim to divine authority and how he uses the father-son metaphor to explain his relationship with God. How does this concept resonate with the people of his time, and why does it irritate the religious leaders so much?

Finally, I want to know why the Roman authorities also see Jesus as a threat. What exactly makes them decide to execute him? Do they view his teachings as a political insurgency? I am eager to understand the broader social and political implications of Jesus' ministry and why it leads to such a drastic response from the ruling powers.

"Christ Blessing the Children," painted between 1620-1625 by Artemisia Gentileschi. This painting depicts Jesus blessing a group of children, illustrating the biblical narrative from the Gospel of Matthew (Chapter 19, verses 13-15) where Jesus welcomes children and emphasizes the importance of childlike faith in the kingdom of God, reflecting themes of love, acceptance, and the inclusivity of Jesus' teachings.

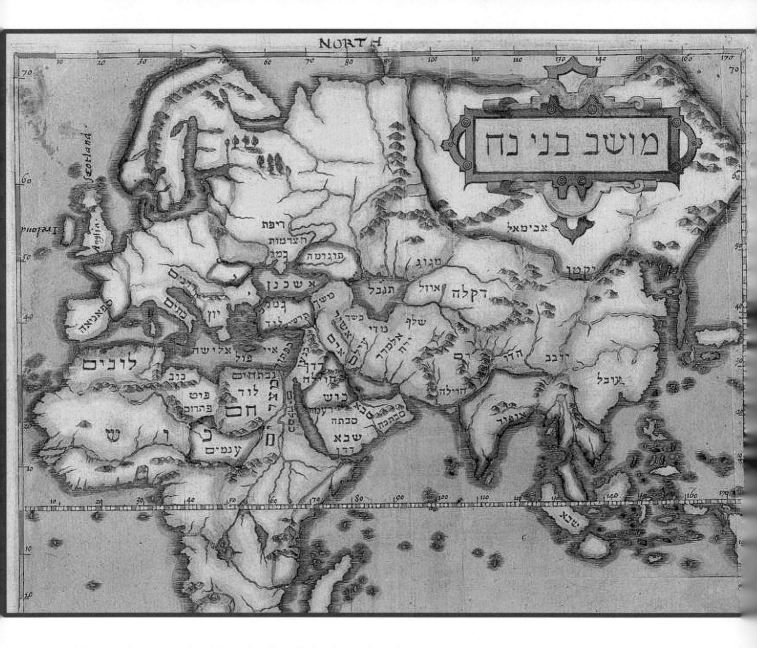

Allen, what was the historical, political, and social context of Palestine during the time of Jesus, particularly regarding the regional divisions and Roman authority?

It was a period of flux. It was a period of great tension. It was a period of political transition. And we can view Jesus' activity historically as being significant. Palestine was divided up in about four different parts. Judea, to the far south, and Samaria, the midsection of the country, were being ruled directly by Roman authority in Jesus' time. Galilee is Jesus' stomping grounds in the first three Gospels and they make a big deal of Jesus' Galilean activity. That's being ruled by one of Herod the Great's sons, as is the region sort of on the other side of the Jordan.

All of these regions are ancestral regions of Israel, but they're under different authorities. And the relations between these authorities is problematic. The relations of all these authorities with the people is problematic. And there's a lot of tension. Then, on top of all of this, there's Roman imperialism. The Romans are running the show in the Eastern Mediterranean. This is causing

103

what we would call development. We get some big cities on the kind of Greco-Roman pattern or the Greek cities.

A lot of wealth is being concentrated in the urban areas. Whenever that happens, what's really happening is that that stuff is being drained from the countryside. Pressure is being exerted on those agrarian populations to produce more and more surplus to pay more and more taxes to pay for theaters that they don't attend. To pay for games and amusements that they can't afford. Palaces that they don't live in. And that causes a lot of tension.

More and more people are becoming poorer and poorer. This is a problem in first-century Palestine. The wealthy people are becoming wealthier. And that wealth has achieved a level of ostentation and arrogance that's just a bit too much to bear.

Huston, what was the experience and perspective of the Jewish people living under Roman rule during the time of Jesus?

They were an oppressed people, heavily oppressed under the heel of the Roman boot. And, therefore, they desperately longed for an improvement in their situation, which they realized, since they were a minuscule group with no power could not come through their own devices, would have to come through divine intervention. But they had a part to play, and that part was to listen to what Yahweh God had told them, namely, "Ye shall be a holy people." And they had set up standards as to what that holiness involved, such as dietary laws and not working on the Sabbath, things like that. And so, their hope was that if they lived up to the law perfectly, then God would say, okay, you've done your part. I will do mine and I will intervene and overthrow the Roman yoke, release you from the Roman yoke.

Allen, what was the nature of Roman rule in Palestine, including their motivations and actions, and how did the local population, with their tradition of political autonomy, react to their subjugation and loss of independence?

The Romans came to rule Palestine. They came to take the people's wealth, and they came to live in splendor. And they came to say that their gods had given them dominion over all of the inhabitable earth, the earth that they knew at the time. Then there are these people in Palestine with a tradition of political autonomy. Now they've fallen on hard times. They never really accept their fate, their political fate.

It's in that context of tension that the people are having this collective memory of political autonomy and freedom. Not all the time, but there are great moments. Under King David's monarchy, for example, the people aspired to revisit those great days and get these other foreigners off their necks. And they believe not only were they politically autonomous at one

"King David, the King of Israel," painted in 1622 by Gerard van Honthorst. This painting portrays King David, a significant figure in the Old Testament, known for his leadership, psalms, and covenant with God, as described in various chapters of the Bible including Samuel, and Psalms, highlighting themes of kingship, faith, and divine favor.

time, but that God had ordained that. And Jesus' activity is redolent with all these aspirations. We can't really understand it very well without seeing it in the context of those expectations.

There are traditions that say that when the bottom really falls out, God is going to send somebody to fix things. Or God's going to do something dramatic to fix things. And the kinds of things He's going to do are very much sort of kind of like things He's done before. And so we find that in Jesus' time about a dozen instances of charismatic prophetic leaders showing up and doing weird kinds of things and things that look weird unless you understand the tradition.

Richard, how did Jesus' approach to religious law and human nature differ from that of the scribes and Pharisees, and what impact did this have on the established religious practices of the time?

We said the law had to be very complex because people were very simple. Here's what Jesus does. Jesus respects the infinite complexity of the human person. Every person seems to be a unique creation of God, who break the rules in their own way. Jesus honors that and respects that people are very complex, and therefore he makes the law very simple. Jesus basically says, love God and love your neighbor. Well, this, I mean, this just put the scribes and the Pharisees and the elders out of business, you know? They had a whole brokerage system of the hoops you had to jump and how you got your sins forgiven. And here is this layman, which Jesus was, a Jewish uneducated layman, telling him, your sins are forgiven.

Allen, how did Jesus describe his relationship with God, and what cultural or traditional context did he use to explain this relationship to his followers?

Jesus talked about God as his father. And that his working in the world was very much like the agency that we see in the relationship between the son and the father. In all traditional societies, the son is really the extension of the father. And in many traditional societies, the son does what the father did. He learns his craft or skill of the way he makes his living from his father. He just hangs out with him and learns. And then as his father goes on his reward, the son goes on to do what the father once did. Even when the father's alive, the son is basically just a reflection of the father's authority and draws upon that to do what he does. Jesus used this as a metaphor apparently in his own ministry to explain his agency. "I'm doing what I'm doing down here just as my father in Heaven does what he does up there.

If you consider the traditional metaphor of the father-son relationship it has a kind of homespun quality about it. At the same time, it is implicitly subversive. It has a kind of very sharp theological edge to it. So that if you're in the habit of quoting the great sages, or of talking about this particular tradition, or that particular tradition, then someone comes along and says I've got it from God that it's this way. That's quite a trump. And with a trump that powerful, the response is going to be, the response has to be at a very high level. So I think that that part of Jesus' ministry was inherently irritating to his contemporaries because this is quite a trump to play and it's difficult to answer that trump at the level at which it's played.

But some people did try, and this accounts for the invective and the vitriol that we find in a lot of gospel traditions, some of which may not have occurred in Jesus' own time, but may be reflections of later controversies. Controversies that are rooted in this claim to a divine authority.

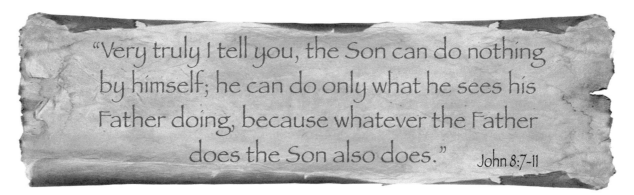

"Very truly I tell you, the Son can do nothing by himself; he can do only what he sees his Father doing, because whatever the Father does the Son also does." John 8:7-11

Allen, What was the significance of Jesus' actions and statements during his outburst in the temple, and how was this event perceived by those who witnessed it?

Jesus' outburst in the temple is one of those pieces of tradition that apparently everyone knew. Jesus violently rearranged the furniture in the temple and says various uncomplimentary things about what was going on there. It was a big deal, but not big enough of a deal for some kind of violent intervention. Jesus was the only violent person in that incident. Clearly, it was a prophetic demonstration, and in the Gospel according to John, Jesus says what people accused him of saying.

In the other three Gospels when Jesus is arrested, one of the charges against him is that he tried to destroy the temple, or he advocated the destruction of the temple. People said that he said that the temple should be destroyed. In the Gospel of John, Jesus says, destroy this temple and I will rebuild it in three days. It comes out of his own mouth. We have other pieces of tradition outside the gospels that corroborate this. The challenge is not whether or not it happened. Nobody is denying that. The incident is recorded in all four of the Gospels. The question is what it means and how do we understand this?

"Christ Cleansing the Temple," painted in 1570 by Domenikos Theotokopoulos, also known as El Greco. This painting depicts the biblical scene from the Gospels of Matthew (Chapter 21, verses 12-13), where Jesus drives out the merchants and money changers from the temple, symbolizing his authority and righteous indignation against religious corruption and exploitation.

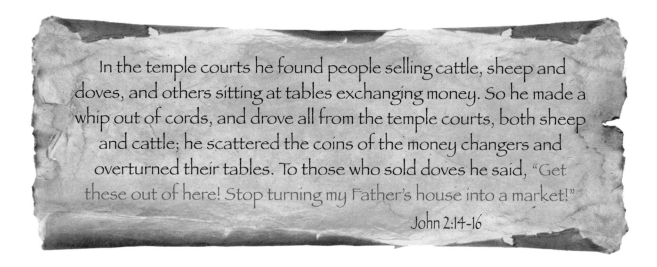

In the temple courts he found people selling cattle, sheep and doves, and others sitting at tables exchanging money. So he made a whip out of cords, and drove all from the temple courts, both sheep and cattle; he scattered the coins of the money changers and overturned their tables. To those who sold doves he said, "Get these out of here! Stop turning my Father's house into a market!"

John 2:14-16

Allen, how did Jesus' activities and teachings respond to the historical issues and criticisms regarding the credibility and conduct of the temple establishment and priestly authorities in Israel?

We can see Jesus against the backdrop of several historical problems to which his activity is a response. The temple establishment had lost its credibility with the people of Israel. There was a lot of complaint among various groups, I'd call dissident intellectuals in Israel, about the temple cult, about the priestly establishment. That they were no longer the mediators of divine grace. That they no longer represented the interest of the people. That they no longer represented God's interests. And that they were enriching themselves at the people's expense.

According to Mosaic Law, they got their cut off the top. They got 10 percent of everything you got. That was a tax you paid that went directly to them. Then there were other taxes on top of that. So you got this priestly establishment that traditionally runs the show. Then on top of that, there's what we would call secular authority. Then on top of that, there's imperial authority. None of those tiers of government are interested in doing anything but taking things from people. And the priestly establishment sometimes is complicit in this kind of systemic ripoff of the people in Palestine. So there's an enormous credibility gap there. He's responding to that.

Allen, what role did the socio-economic conditions of first-century Palestine, particularly widespread hunger and poverty, play in shaping the social dynamics and potential for unrest during that time, and how did Jesus' miracles, particularly those involving food, intersect with these conditions?

Historians have observed that it takes a lot to make a people revolt. The masses, so to speak, generally don't undertake revolutions unless they're really, really desperate. There are a lot of desperate people in Palestine in the first century. People were hungry. We know that Jesus was

"The Arrest of Christ (Kiss of Judas)," painted in 1305 by Giotto di Bondone. This painting portrays the biblical moment from the Gospels of Matthew (Chapter 26, verses 47-50),where Judas Iscariot betrays Jesus with a kiss, leading to his arrest, symbolizing treachery, the fulfillment of prophecy and the beginning of Christ's Passion.

reputed to have practiced miracles that produced food. Food was a big thing for Jesus. I think food is a big thing for anybody who doesn't have it regularly or can't depend on getting it or can't just open the refrigerator and reach in and get it. And there were a lot of people in Palestine that were like that. A lot of people were hungry. A lot of people were poor.

There are pockets of resistance. Places and people and communities, that don't accept things the way they are, and have an alternative vision, and are doing something about that. And that always constitutes a danger to the status quo. And I'm convinced that this is what got Jesus into trouble.

> Judas, one of the Twelve, appeared. With him was a crowd armed with swords and clubs, sent from the chief priests, the teachers of the law, and the elders. Now the betrayer had arranged a signal with them: "The one I kiss is the man; arrest him and lead him away under guard."
>
> Mark 14:43-44

When you've got a bunch of people who are basically running the show, they are responsible for the historical project of the moment. You can only have one of those to a moment. If you have more than one then the two or however many you have are going to be in conflict with each other. The narrative implication is that Jesus called attention to himself, and this is the engine that drove the temple establishment to finally come against him.

In modern scholarship, there's been a big debate historically about whether he was or wasn't just a preacher of righteousness. Did he have a political program? If so, was it an insurgent one? Wasn't it a big mistake what he was executed for? I don't think it was a mistake. I think the Romans knew exactly what they were doing. They discerned the presence of a troublemaker who was sending some kind of social shockwave across his neighborhood. The Romans didn't care why. They didn't care what kind of God he worshipped. They didn't care what kind of traditions he was trying to reactivate. All they knew was he was talking about a kingdom that wasn't theirs. And you only get one kingdom to a customer. So he had to go.

Reflections

Allen vividly describes a turbulent period in ancient Palestine during Jesus' time. He portrays the deep-seated regional divisions and tensions among various authorities governing Israelite territories, including Roman imperialism and the Temple Cult, much of it arising from the economic pressures squeezing the population. Rome's presence coincides with the concentration of wealth and power in urban centers, while rural areas are pressured to produce an excessive surplus for taxes and luxurious indulgences that primarily benefit the elite.

Jesus walks straight into this tinderbox with a subversive message that directly challenges the arrogance and disparity of the ruling class. The Jesus Movement emerges as a transformative force against systemic injustice, offering hope and solidarity to those enduring hardship and exclusion, creating tension.

The Temple Cult quickly recognizes a threat to its authority. While they emphasize intricate rules and extract money from the masses, Jesus simplifies the law to its essence: love for God and love for one's neighbor. This challenges entrenched religious hierarchies and legalistic systems that are the arbiters of forgiveness and spiritual access. This approach democratizes spirituality and emphasizes personal connection with God, bypassing the Temple Cult and affirming the individual's unique relationship with divine grace, further heightening tension in the region.

Jesus begins teaching and spreading his message with unprecedented authority, claiming a direct connection to God as his father. As Allen describes, Jesus' metaphor of himself as the son carrying out God's will directly undercuts the cult's reliance on priests for mediation and rituals. Jesus' message is viewed as a clear and present danger that is also gathering momentum.

In his defense Jesus said to them, "My Father is always at his work to this very day, and I too am working." For this reason, they tried all the more to kill him; not only was he breaking the Sabbath, but he was even calling God his own Father, making himself equal with God. (John 5:17-19)

It is hard to argue that Jesus' actions in the temple sealed his fate. By overturning tables, disrupting commercial activities, and denouncing the exploitation of worship for profit, he exposed the naked hypocrisy within the religious establishment. His assertion that he would rebuild the temple in three days, understood as a reference to his resurrection, undermined the temple's centrality in Jewish religious life and suggested a new spiritual paradigm. This could not stand.

As Allen points out, this act was not just a symbolic protest but a deliberate challenge to the religious elite's control over spiritual practices. By condemning the exploitation and corruption within the temple cult, Jesus exposed the systemic injustices perpetuated by religious and secular authorities alike. His critique of the priestly establishment, which profited from religious taxes and collaborations with imperial powers, undermined their claim to divine authority and exposed their complicity in oppressing the people. Jesus' subversive actions were seen by all as a revolutionary call for social and spiritual reform.

Allen highlights how the region was rife with desperation due to widespread hunger and poverty, making people more susceptible to revolutionary ideas. Jesus' miracles, particularly those that provided food, directly addressed these critical needs, making his ministry especially relevant to the oppressed masses. His alignment with pockets of resistance, communities rejecting the status quo, positioned him as a direct threat to existing power structures.

By preaching about a different kind of kingdom—one not under Roman control—Jesus implicitly challenged the legitimacy of Roman authority and the temple's complicity in systemic exploitation. The Romans' decision to execute him was a strategic move to eliminate this threat. Allen's line addressing this is my favorite in the film: "All they knew was he was talking about a kingdom that wasn't theirs. And you only get one kingdom to a customer. So he had to go."

To follow are twelve engravings that vividly depict Jesus' outburst in the temple to his crucifixion. I was fortunate to have been able to photograph these powerful works at the Harvard Divinity School while interviewing Allen Callahan. These images were used in a scene in the film Portrait of a Radical to great effect.

The series "Vita, Passio, et Resurrectio Iesu Christi" translates to "The Life, Passion, and Resurrection of Jesus Christ." It is a thematic grouping of artworks or narratives that depict key events from the life of Jesus, with a focus on his teachings, his suffering and death (the Passion), and his resurrection. This thematic series is central to Christian theology and art, as it encompasses the core tenets of the Christian faith. "Vita" refers to his life and ministry, including his teachings, miracles, and interactions with followers. "Passio" encompasses the events leading up to and including Jesus' crucifixion. "Resurrectio" depicts the miraculous resurrection of Jesus from the dead, Adriaen Collaert published the series in Antwerp around 1598. The original artist who illustrated the series was Maarten de Vos (1532-1603).

Above - Christ driving the money changers from the temple.

Below - The arrest of Christ and the healing of Malchus ear.

Christ standing before the high-priest Caiaphas.

Christ standing before the Pontius Pilate.

Christ standing before Herod.

The flagellation of Christ.

Christ being crowned with thorns.
Christ presented to a large crowd as King of the Jews.

Pilate seated washing his hands as Christ is lead away by soldiers.

Christ carrying the cross on the road to Calvary.

Christ being nailed to the cross.

Christ crucified between the two thieves.

In this section of the film, I am driven by a desire to gain a more in-depth understanding of the circumstances surrounding Jesus' crucifixion and the profound suffering he endured. How did the Romans settle on the use of crucifixion to maintain order and instill fear in the population? We have all seen images depicting the crucifixion, but I'm not sure how many of us have tried to fully imagine the mental and physical pain a person was suffering. And what of the diverse reactions of the crowd witnessing such events—some mourning, others cheering?

I am also curious about St. Bonaventure's perspective on Jesus' crucifixion as a "collision of opposites," which Richard Rohr has written about. How does St. Bonaventure's perspective on Jesus' crucifixion as a collision of opposites shed light on the profound significance of Jesus' mission to reconcile opposing forces? How does this understanding deepen our comprehension of Jesus' role as the embodiment of divine reconciliation, bridging the gap between humanity and God, and between conflicting aspects of existence? Moreover, what implications arise from the fact that Jesus' mission was frequently misunderstood and met with rejection from various quarters? How does this narrative of misunderstanding and rejection resonate with contemporary experiences of striving for unity and reconciliation in a world marked by division and conflict?

"St. Bonaventure,"1890, by Rebecca Orpen. He was a 13ᵗʰ Century Franciscan friar and theologian, renowned for his influential writings and profound contributions to medieval philosophy and theology.

Finally, I want to understand the profound significance behind Jesus' death and resurrection, especially considering the brutal nature of his crucifixion. How can we see anything good about Good Friday when in fact it seems to represent the absence of hope? And how are we to contrast this with Jesus' resurrection? One portrays suffering and death, while the other celebrates resurrection and victory. How does understanding Good Friday illuminate the significance of Easter Sunday?

"Christ Leaving the Court," 1874, by Gustave Doré depicts Jesus being led away after his trial before Pontius Pilate, highlighting his calm resignation amidst injustice. This scene relates to the Gospel of Matthew, specifically Matthew 27:1-2, where Pilate washes his hands of Jesus' fate and hands him over to be crucified.

Allen, what were the circumstances surrounding Jesus' death, and how did the manner in which he was executed reflect not only the physical pain involved but also the broader significance of public execution as a tool of state terror?

Jesus' death was a horrible death. It was the most horrible death you could die in antiquity. It was horrible not only because it was painful. It was excruciatingly painful. But because it was public. It was an act of degradation. This was not just a way of executing a criminal. This was a way of terrorizing a population. You take someone who has abrogated your rules and you make him a billboard of state terror. And that's what happened to Jesus. He is publicly tortured to death on the cross.

We don't know who invented this form of torture. Some people think it came from the east. But even if the Romans didn't invent it, once they got it, they refined it. It was just one specimen of their technical expertise. They were good at things like that. Building roads, organizing armies, executing people. This was a way of showing subject population what happens when you transgress the Roman order.

It was a painful death. It was an ignominious death. It was a death of disgrace and such people were public spectacles. They were afforded no grace or mercy. Executed naked usually, and then just left to die in the sun. This was the death that Jesus suffered because of the sentence that was declared. He was convicted as a criminal for acts against the Roman state.

Richard, you've spoken of St. Bonaventure and his characterization of Jesus' crucifixion as a convergence of opposing forces. Could you explain that?

St. Bonaventure, our Franciscan mystic, said that Jesus was killed on the collision of opposites. He was crucified on the coincidence of opposites. That he hangs there wherever oppositional energy comes together, of this group and that group. And he gives his life to reconcile the two sides.

Whenever you try to build a bridge between two sides, I always say they'll walk on you from both sides. You'll be misunderstood by both sides. You're not in either group. That's the naked position of Jesus. The naked position of the gospel which I don't think is ever going to be popular. I don't think it's ever going to fill stadiums.

Allen, why is the crucifixion and resurrection of Jesus considered so significant in Christianity, particularly in terms of transforming despair into hope, even in the face of seemingly insurmountable adversity?

The crucifixion and the resurrection of Jesus is so important for the Christian faith because it

121

"Golgotha," 1900, Edvard Munch. This painting portrays the agony of Christ's crucifixion at Golgotha, emphasizing the emotional suffering and existential turmoil, which can be associated with Jesus' cry of abandonment in Matthew 27:46, where he exclaims, "My God, my God, why have you forsaken me?" Munch's expressionist style intensifies the scene's emotional impact, reflecting the profound despair and isolation described in the Bible.

means, first of all, that there is a Good Friday that's really not that good at all. Where hope just can't be found. It's not that you can't see it. It's not there. It's really not there. But your incapacity to hope doesn't stop the hope. It's like a hope beyond hope.

So, in the Gospels, on the first Easter, nobody believed that he was going to beat that. Nobody believed that it was possible. Now, he's been saying this, at least according to gospel tradition, this is going to happen so be ready for it, be prepared. The things we're going to go through are going to be very difficult, so be prepared. When it happened, it was such a disastrous finish to what was such a glorious beginning. That was such a disaster that no human hope could sustain it. And so, everyone's heart was broken.

122

Richard, how does the concept of God in Jesus challenge the human desire for definitive solutions and remedies to the complexities and paradoxes of existence?

Ironically, God in Jesus ends up not being the cure or the fix for the human paradox. And that's what we want. We want answers. We want something to explain it all. In real truth, Jesus is the one who leads us into the dilemma. It leads us into the paradox. It teaches you how to hold the opposites, the tension. It's no accident, even in the image of his crucifixion, that he hangs between heaven and earth, between a good thief and a bad thief, a masculine body with a feminine soul. It's like this Jesus figure hanging between heaven and earth, divine and human for us Christians. Holding together the ultimate opposites that name our souls. That's the dilemma for all of us.

"Crucifixion," created between 1457-1460 by Andrea Mantegna. This painting depicts the biblical event of Jesus' crucifixion, as described in the Gospels of Matthew (Chapter 27, verses 32-56), symbolizing the central Christian belief in Jesus' sacrificial death for the redemption of humanity.

Allen, what evidence exists regarding Jesus' death and the subsequent reports of his resurrection, particularly concerning the certainty of his death and the claims of sightings by his followers?

Jesus' body's broken, and he is humiliated to death. Then three days later, there are rumors that he's alive. Now the traditions are very emphatic about two things: that he died. It's clear that he died. The traditions are very precise about this. He didn't swoon; it wasn't a coma; he was dead. He was dead, and the body was taken away. Then, when people were searching for the body, it was gone. What follows are explanations of this. What happened to the body? The followers say that he got up and walked away from it. "Well, how do you know that? Because we saw him." About 25 years later, when the Apostle Paul is writing about this to the Corinthians, he said that several people saw Jesus after his execution. He said at one point, maybe about 500 people saw him. So a lot of people in the community saw Jesus after what became a community after his execution.

> ...he appeared to Cephas, then to the twelve. Then he appeared to more than five hundred brothers at one time, most of whom are still alive, though some have fallen asleep. Then he appeared to James, then to all the apostles. Last of all, as to one untimely born, he appeared also to me. Corinthians 15:5-8

Allen, what theological challenges arise from the belief among Jesus' followers that he survived the ordeal of his brutal crucifixion, and how does this belief reflect a deeper understanding of divine power and resilience?

There's one element here that I think is compelling, and this is the most problematic. This is where theologians rush in where angels fear to tread. The whole business about the death and resurrection. His followers believed that he died, but that somehow he survived that ordeal. The horrible, very undignified, ignominious death. The excruciating public torture. Somehow he beat that. And that this too was a sign that whatever it was he was doing couldn't be stopped. God was in it and could make a comeback, even from the grave.

There are a lot of things it could mean. One of the things it means is that here is a person who was realizing in some way in his actions the aspirations of a people. He's brutally executed. But even that doesn't stop him. Paul looks back on the tradition of Jesus' resurrection, and he refers to Jesus as the first fruits. That is, he's the first wave of the harvest of a multitude of people who will enjoy victory over death. And he writes this to the Corinthians and says you comfort each other with these words. It doesn't mean that we're not going to face death. Paul wrote that. He reminded the Corinthians of that victory over death precisely because they were facing death because some of their members had already died.

There were some people at Corinth who were thinking that because Jesus had been raised from the dead because they had put their trust in Jesus, they wouldn't have to die. They wouldn't have to face mortality. Paul says no. He says this gives you the strength to face mortality because you know that it's not the end. He says this is our hope. There are people who really experience it at the gravesite when that loved one passes away. We cannot obviate that pain, but we can triumph over it, we can transcend it. Jesus matters because in him we see the story of God beating all the odds. That God will do the impossible. That's his forte. God is good at that. And that God will do that. And God will do that on our behalf when we are working with God. God calls us to work with him. And as we do so, God will make things happen for us that sometimes we can't even believe what happened. God will do the unbelievable even when we can't believe it.

Reflections

The Romans use crucifixion not just to kill but to humiliate and terrorize. As Allen frames it, this public spectacle serves as a stark warning to anyone who might challenge Roman authority. It is a tool of imperial control. It isn't just about physical suffering; it is about the complete degradation and dehumanization of someone considered a threat. By making an example of Jesus, the Romans aim to instill fear and suppress dissent among the population. Perhaps the Romans miscalculated in Jesus' case because by enduring this most shameful and painful death, he becomes a powerful symbol of resistance against oppressive powers, revealing the lengths to which the authorities would go to maintain control and suppress revolutionary ideas such as those that animate the Jesus Movement.

Father Rohr makes a particularly interesting observation in St. Bonaventure's metaphorical interpretation of Jesus' crucifixion as occurring at the "collision of opposites." This imagery powerfully conveys the idea that Jesus' death is not merely a physical event but a profound act of reconciliation. By positioning Jesus at the intersection of conflicting forces, Bonaventure highlights the spiritual significance of his sacrifice as an attempt to bridge deep divisions. He goes on to describe Jesus' crucifixion as the ultimate act of reconciliation, where he absorbs the hostility and misunderstandings of opposing groups, suggesting that true peacemaking, or forgiveness, which is central to Jesus' message, requires immense sacrifice and often leads to being misunderstood and rejected by all sides involved. It reflects the reality that efforts to reconcile differences often meet with resistance and hostility from those entrenched in their positions.

The juxtaposition of despair and hope in the context of Jesus' crucifixion and resurrection is stark.

"Christ's Apparition to the Disciples," 1613-1615, Sebastiano Ricci. This painting depicts the moment when the resurrected Jesus appears to his disciples, a scene that can be interpreted as a powerful confirmation of Jesus' resurrection and divine nature as described in the Bible. This event is detailed in the Gospel of John, chapter 20, where Jesus shows his wounds to the doubting Thomas, affirming his identity and resurrection.

Allen points out the notion that Good Friday is a day that "isn't really good at all." Yet it ultimately leads to the resurrection, which embodies a profound paradox central to the Christian faith. The disciples' disbelief and heartbreak following Jesus' death highlight and the seeming finality of his crucifixion underscore the miraculous nature of the resurrection. It serves as a powerful reminder that even in the darkest moments, when all seems lost and no human hope remains, divine intervention can bring about unimaginable renewal and redemption.

What I find particularly interesting is the paradoxical nature Rohr points out of Jesus' role. Instead of being the "answer" to the human condition, he exemplifies how to navigate the inherent tensions and contradictions of life. The imagery of Jesus hanging on the cross between heaven and earth, and between a good thief and a bad thief, symbolizes the intersection of divine and human realms, and the coexistence of good and evil. I had never sifted that out of either the gospels or their many depictions in art. This perspective shifts the focus from seeking straightforward resolutions to understanding the importance of enduring and reconciling life's dualities. It emphasizes the spiritual maturity required to hold and integrate opposites, reflecting a more profound and nuanced approach to faith and existence. Jesus' crucifixion becomes a metaphor for this spiritual balancing act.

Jesus' resurrection is not just about a miraculous return to life but represents the enduring nature of the aspirations and beliefs that Jesus embodies. His resurrection becomes a powerful symbol of resilience and the undying spirit of the Jesus movement, suggesting that even the most extreme attempts to suppress or destroy a profound truth or hope will ultimately fail. That spirit to rise from the ashes and carry on the movement is most profoundly exemplified in the later actions of his disciples, who face severe persecution for their faith, with many suffering martyrdom through various brutal means such as crucifixion, beheading, and stoning, all the while succeeding in spreading Jesus' profound and subversive message across different regions.

In this final section of the film, I pose very general questions to allow the participants to express what comes up naturally, providing a canvas for their unfiltered thoughts and reflections. The themes we explore revolve around the multifaceted interpretations and profound implications of Jesus' teachings.

This open-ended approach is designed to capture the diverse perspectives and personal connections they have with the teachings of Jesus. It allows us to delve into the rich tapestry of meanings that these teachings hold for different people, influenced by their unique experiences, backgrounds, and spiritual journeys.

Allen, how have Jesus' words been used and misused over time, evolving from their profound impact during his life to carrying an aura of authority that is often appropriated by various groups?

That Jesus' words are often misused is, I think, undeniable; no one could argue against that. That Jesus' words have been appropriated, expropriated, used by so many people. His words carry authority now. His words are now larger than life. They were profound. They had an extraordinary effect on people in their own time. Now they've taken on this aura of authority. When you have some people saying that there was a man in first-century Palestine who was actually God, that adds a lot of authority to anything he said or did.

Anybody who wants to do anything wants to expropriate that authority if they can. This is a game that everybody plays. You find an authority and then you manipulate it for your own ends. So we can expect Jesus' words to be bent and twisted and stolen and used by all kinds of people.

One of the things that constantly revives the tradition is a return to Jesus, and I think that is why there's a perennial interest in Jesus. Among other things, he's a touchstone for the authenticity of the tradition. His words carry an inherent critique of the tradition itself. His words constantly keep the tradition honest. And people are coming back to that. That's why they were really remembered in the first place. Jesus' words were a way for the community to help struggle to keep itself honest.

"Head of Christ," 1648, Rembrandt van Rijn. This painting portrays a contemplative and expressive image of Jesus. Rembrandt often depicted biblical figures with deep humanity and emotional depth. This painting represents Christ, capturing his compassion and serenity, and emphasizing the intimate and personal nature of religious devotion.

Richard, how might Christianity have been different if Jesus had been understood primarily as an example of what it means to be human, rather than as a means to attain heaven?

It's been said that we are human beings trying to become spiritual and what Jesus is personifying is that we're already spiritual beings and the problem is really how to become human. For me, Jesus personifies the quintessential human being. I think Jesus operates in history almost as a divine lure, pulling our humanity out of ourselves, pulling us forward, attracting us, seducing us, if you will, into an ever more attractive humanity.

I think if we had read Jesus as, "Here's what it means to be human," instead of, "Here's the way to get to heaven," we would have had a much less contentious Christianity. A much less ideological, heady Christianity. Arguing about who's right and who's got right answers to the divine SAT test. It's basically a waste of time because it simply feeds the ego. But if we can see Jesus as the human one, this is what a real mensch, a real human being would look like at its best.

I believe Jesus, despite our best attempts to stop him, is exercising that function in human history very slowly because we're resisting him in every way we can. We want to make him the divine savior of our denomination. And so we spend a great deal of time worshiping him and proving that he is God. Whereas the most common word he uses for Himself, by far more than any other term is this strange term that we've translated as "Son of Man." It really means son of a human being, one of you, every man. He's always calling himself "Every Man." The quintessential human being. "I'm what it means to be human. Just look at me and trust it."

Huston, how does the concept of the incarnation, where God becomes human, relate to the idea that humans are created in the image of God, and what implications does this hold for the potential transformation of humanity?

One of the ways in which the early church summed up the miracle of the incarnation was that God became man so that man might become God. God became human so that humans can become God. And I think that does say it. However, there was an antecedent. In the Book of Genesis, when it comes to the creation story and the creation of the human being, the terminology is "I will create man in my own image." Now, that means God being divine, I will create man as divine. That image makes a slight difference because the finite can never become totally human. It's like the mountain at the bottom of the lake. It is a reflection. So, we're told at the very start that we are divine. Not 100%, but 99.44. It's there. The divinity is within us. The problem is simply that it's become overlaid with so much crud, and selfishness, and guilt, fear, anger, and ego. A lamp can have a flame inside, but whatever is covering can be overlaid with first dust and then dirt and then mud and finally, you can get to the point that no light is visible at all. And in the people who

"But that you may know that the Son of Man has authority on earth to forgive sins…"

Matthew 8:20

Jesus replied, "Foxes have holes and birds of the air have nests, but the Son of Man has no place to lay his head."

Matthew 9:16

"For the Son of Man is Lord of the Sabbath."

Matthew 12:8

When Jesus came to the region of Caesarea Philippi, he asked his disciples, "Who do people say the Son of Man is?"

Matthew 16:13

"But I say to all of you: From now on you will see the Son of Man sitting at the right hand of the Mighty One and coming on the clouds of heaven."

Matthew 26:64

"For the Son of Man came to save the lost."

Matthew 18:11

seem to be just inherently evil, why that is not a bad analogy for what has happened.

Within Christianity, there emerged the phrase "In Adam's fall, we sinned all." We're fallen creatures, which is another way of saying we're mixed bags. Divine at base, but with a great overlay of fallibility and ignorance and error. This is our natural tendency if we're immature. But if we develop character along the way, why then the emphasis changes from give me beatitude, give me heaven as the raw reward for my good deeds, to what we can give to the world here and to God. Rabia, a great woman Sufi saint in Islam, put it beautifully. She said, "If I love you and Allah in Islam for the hope of heaven, please keep me out of heaven. And if I love you out of the fear of hell, please send me to hell. But if I love you for your own sake, then please admit me to your presence." But the point is that the divinity is right here and can be accessed. And in the Father's way of putting it, the impact of Jesus was to access that divinity which is already there, and to let it shine forth.

Richard, how does the concept of "veiling" great truths that you've written about relate to the transformative power of significant life experiences, and how does religion prepare individuals to embrace and be changed by these moments?

All great truths must be veiled. The big truths are simply too much for the psyche at any one moment. That's probably why we have theater. It's probably why we have art. It's probably why

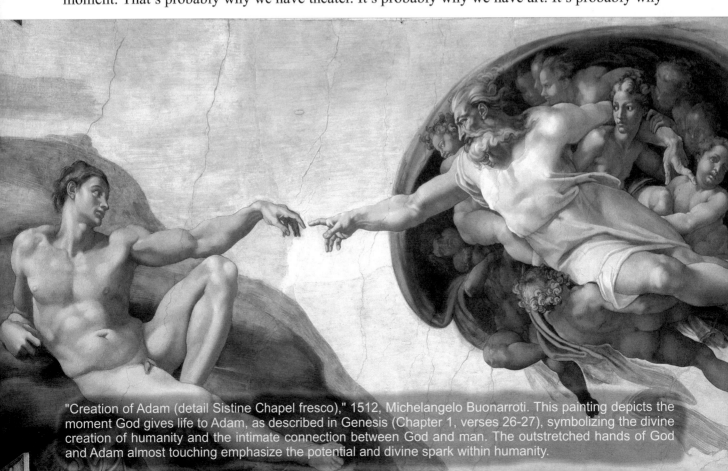

"Creation of Adam (detail Sistine Chapel fresco)," 1512, Michelangelo Buonarroti. This painting depicts the moment God gives life to Adam, as described in Genesis (Chapter 1, verses 26-27), symbolizing the divine creation of humanity and the intimate connection between God and man. The outstretched hands of God and Adam almost touching emphasize the potential and divine spark within humanity.

God draws our life out over 70 years or 80 if we are strong, as the psalmist says. We can only take the great truths in little doses. It's things like unconditional love, birth, and death that transform us. These are the things that open the soul and change you forever. Those are the great truths, and you're normally never ready for them. What great religion is doing is readying the soul. Sort of tilling the soil. So that when these great moments happen, you know how to look. You know how to feel. You know how to experience it. You know how to let it transform you.

They say that most of the literature and operas and poetry of the world are all about two things. They're all about love and death. Because there's really nothing else to talk about. And once you hear that, it becomes sort of obvious. Every great piece of literature is about love and death. Because those are the only two things that really transform us. And we're constantly trying to get a handle on them because they're too big. So we just get them in little doses and little pieces. And I think that's what the work of religion should be. Sort of readying the soul, so that when the spirit shows itself you're ready to say, this is great. This is God. This is everything. This is what I've been waiting for.

I think that's the work of religion. Whereas what we do so often, at least in my church, is we give little kids the big answers in the first grade, and they think they have God as their private property in their pocket. They've already got the big answers. So there's no readiness, there's no expectation that at most they got a little, tiny, tiny fragment of the great mystery. I think healthy religion keeps you humble. And what unhealthy religion does is make you very arrogant, makes you think you got it already. You've got the great mystery. Healthy religion says, no you've barely touched upon it. I haven't even begun.

Richard, how does fundamentalism, present in various world religions, contrast with the traditional spiritual journey characterized by embracing complexity, uncertainty, and the quest for deeper understanding?

Fundamentalism is found in all the great world religions. Where the spiritual journey is no longer a journey into the dark night of the soul. The desperate journey for God. It's having happy little answers and being absolutely sure about them. So you never have to suffer humiliation. You never have to suffer insecurity. And I can see why the ego wants that. But that really is not mature religion. It almost feels as if we're dumbing down on some levels. And maybe it's because the world is too complex. That the human person wants to be certain about something. I wish I could say that God offers us that. But I don't have any evidence in the Bible that God is offering us a little plate of certitudes. It seems that God is instead offering us a dark, and dangerous, and wonderful journey toward God. He's offering us faith, not certitude. And one of the greatest heresies, if I can call it that, in the history of Christianity is, we turn the meaning of faith absolutely around to mean the exact opposite.

Jesus seemed to be calling us out of our comfort zones. Get out of your boats. Cross the shore onto the other side where the pagans live. Always taking people where they didn't want to go. And we turned it around and we have made religion into people who don't have to go to any place new because we've got everything right here at home. And it simply doesn't create great people. It doesn't create people who can build bridges. It doesn't create people who can understand. It doesn't create people who have compassion. It doesn't create a people of forgiveness or understanding.

Huston, how has the rise of modern science challenged traditional religious worldviews, particularly in societies where secularism has become increasingly prominent, and what role does the scientific method play in shaping contemporary understandings of the transcendent and human existence?

There has been no society in human history that has been as aggressively secular as ours has. One of the reasons for that is that prior to the rise of modern science, all societies were religious. And that meant, ultimately, that they saw themselves as having been created by God. So the transcendent, or that which is greater than the human, was the ultimate, and we are the derivative therefrom.

Now, with the rise of modern science, that traditional worldview was challenged by the scientific worldview, which, as we know, has enormous power because the crux of the scientific method is the controlled experiment, and therefore the scientists have proof. We religious people have no proof. We have insight. I'm not going to lower my self-esteem and just give it all over to the scientists because they've got proof. We have insight, but we do not have proof on the material level. But it has been so mind-boggling, so awesome. I mean, putting people on the moon. How can you not just fall down in salams and praise for that?

However, the material is only a part. It's only like icebergs in the sea of spirit. It doesn't help us to blind ourselves to the fact that there's a real competition going on in our society. Who has the window onto the big picture? The traditional, the religious, or the scientific? Science can deal with part of the picture, whereas religion deals with the whole. Now that sounds like it's giving me the benefit because I deal with a wider terrain, which I think is true. But I will immediately say I cannot deal with that precision. The exactness that science can handle in its smoke.

Now that's been a long way around to the first half of your question. Why is Jesus and Christianity, and for that matter, all of the religions–why do their defects loom before us more than their virtues? I'm not above saying that that's because there is a war of the worlds and the scientists have the ear of the elite in our society because the universities are ruled by the scientific worldview today and they put the finishing touches on the people who go out to rule our society.

Christit in the Storm on the Sea of Galilee," 1695, Ludolf Bakhuizen. This painting portrays Jesus calming the stormy waters of the Sea of Galilee, surrounded by his terrified disciples, mirroring the Biblical account of divine intervention and faith in Mark 4:35-41. The dramatic depiction emphasizes the power of Jesus' presence and command, offering a visual representation of faith's ability to bring peace amidst chaos.

"Taking of Jerusalem by the Crusaders," 1847, Émile Signol. This painting depicts the moment when Crusaders captured Jerusalem in 1099, symbolizing the intense religious fervor and the belief in reclaiming the Holy City for Christianity, which is significant in biblical prophecy (Psalm 122:6-9).

And so enemies, I don't like warfare language, but I don't like to cover up this point either, seldom have the best view of the other side. In academia, it goes by a technical phrase, "the hermeneutics of suspicion." The interpreting things with a suspicious eye. And that's the way the elite in our society have turned to viewing our traditions–seeing the mistakes of which there are oceans of them. The bad thing is not in seeing the mistake, but in not seeing the virtues.

There is a lot of animosity towards religions and religious institutions. I find that I want to cast the ounces of my mind or my strength on defending them. Not by any means for everything they've done. We get nowhere by just closing out the dark side of the picture. There have been sins aplenty. This touches on a point about the difference between spirituality and religion. As a teacher, I have never found a student who did not feel that he or she had a spiritual side to their nature. Spirituality is a good word on campus. Religion is not a good word on campus. What's the difference? Religion is institutionalized spirituality.

That's how I take it. My students like it when I talk about spirituality and the human spirit and things like that. But when I get into defending institutions, why then I've got an argument that I have to make. What I try to get them to see is that institutions are inevitably a mixed bag. A lot of my students, the traditions that they grew up in rubbed them the wrong way. I think of them as wounded Christians, or wounded Jews. And I can understand that very, very well. It just happened that I think of myself as having been fortunate. They think about Christianity in terms of two things: dogmatism and moralism. Dogmatism, we've got the truth, everybody else is going to hell. Moralism, don't do this, that, or the other thing, especially not the other thing. Now that's the way it impacted them.

With me, it was entirely different. It wasn't dogmatism or moralism at all. It was, we're in good hands, and in gratitude for that fact. It would be well if we bore one another's burden. And in all of my gallivanting around the world, I still haven't found a simple formula that tops that one.

Richard, how has the misuse of sacred texts contributed to violence, prejudice, and enmity throughout history, and what role should spiritual texts ideally play in fostering humility, curiosity, and open-mindedness?

We probably don't know how to read sacred literature. I think the Bible has done more damage in human history than probably any other book. It's been used to justify more violence, more prejudice, more enmity, more vengeance than probably any other book. The very best thing is also the very worst thing. People who already think they're spiritual are almost always going to abuse sacred texts because they use them as power. They use them as righteousness. They use them as a way of being in control, a way of being more right or more saved. Whereas what spiritual texts should really do is keep us always with what I like to call a beginner's mind. An awareness that I'm just starting, and this is merely parting the veil for a moment. It doesn't give you certitude, it gives you curiosity.

136

"Fall of Man," 1628-29, Peter Paul Rubens. This painting depicts the biblical scene of Adam and Eve eating the forbidden fruit, as described in Genesis (Chapter 3, verses 1-6), symbolizing the original sin and the subsequent fall of humanity from innocence and grace.

In the very beginning of the Bible, in the book of Genesis, the great sin is really a strange kind of sin when you think of it. It doesn't sound like sin at all. The sin is described in Genesis as eating of the tree of the knowledge of good and evil. And that doesn't sound like a sin. Sounds like something that would be good to do. It describes what I would call a lust for answers. A lust for explanation. A lust for certainty. I want to know who's in and who's out, who's right and who's wrong, who's up and who's down, who's gone to heaven and who's gone to hell. That's this eating of the tree of the knowledge of good and evil. God in the Hebrew Scriptures seems to be saying that's a major problem. When you think that you've got all the answers, you stop listening, you stop growing. You stop being transformed.

Huston, what challenges do you face in reconciling the presence of pain, suffering, and natural disasters with the concept of an absolutely perfect being, and what alternative belief or candidate would you consider staking your life on?

H.G. Wells wasn't the most pious man in the world, and once said, "There are only two things

137

that really interested me in life. One is sex, and the other is God." But against that background, I picked up his interest in God. Someone once asked him, "Do you believe in God?" And he groaned and said, "What else?" And I think that resonates with me. Sometimes when we look at all the pain, the suffering, and the natural tragedy, why the notion of it all being under the hand of an absolutely perfect being seems pretty nutty to me too at certain times. But then I come back to H.G. Wells. What else are you going to believe in? And I pose the challenge to anybody else. Just nominate a candidate to stake your life on other than God and it doesn't measure up. I would be happy to publicly debate anyone who wants to give a rival to my candidate.

If you want a hero, now there are others. I think Mahatma Gandhi, the Buddha who is a wonderful rival candidate. But they said very much the same thing in theme. And I also have a very lofty regard for Socrates, who also said much the same thing. But to me, the question is why not? Why not? What are the things that trip you up or trip the public up? If you want to make a case against Christianity, you've got a glorious opportunity. And that's true about any historical religion. If you want to pick up on it that way, you certainly can, and there's evidence. But why pick up on the bad stuff, I happen to like the good stuff better. How would you explain the film that we're doing? We're hoping that the spiritual seeker will get a greater insight as to why Jesus matters.

Richard, what do you think is the fundamental message that Jesus is calling humanity to, regarding both our inherent humanity and the nature of a safe and loving God, and how does this message resonate with individuals regardless of their religious affiliation?

Simone Weil, the wonderful French philosopher, put it very well. She said, "If I would have the choice between falling into the hands of Christ, meaning joining the Church, or falling into the hands of the truth I would sooner just fall into the hands of the truth and God will take it from there." I think that's all Jesus is calling us to. To the truth of our own humanity and the truth of a God who is safe and loving. And that makes it a very safe universe. You don't have to be a Christian to like that. You don't have to be a Christian to be attracted by the beauty of that. And I believe that's Jesus' role in human history. To call humanity forward by the brilliance of his humanity.

Our native peoples here in New Mexico do not even have in their language a word for religion. There's no such word. Because the concept of religion as something separate from the flowers of the field and the relationships between family members doesn't exist. There's only life. And good life is religion. Good life is meeting God. It's all one.

Now this, I believe, is why at the death of Jesus, the Gospels make the point that the temple veil

"The Rending of the Veil," 1869, William Bell Scott. This painting depicts the moment the veil of the temple was torn in two at the death of Jesus, as described in the Gospel of Matthew (Chapter 27, verse 51), symbolizing the end of the separation between God and humanity and the establishment of a new covenant.

tore from top to bottom, which seems like a very dramatic image. But what it's saying is that after Jesus, you can no longer divide the world into the natural and the supernatural, into the sacred and the profane. It's one world, and the temple veil is torn, and the temple has to go. The reason it has to go is because all the world is the temple. Because all the world is sacred for those who've learned how to see. That's a mature religious person. That's my father St. Francis. And that's why he's the patron of ecology and the patron of animals and everything else. Because he knew that he could meet God in nature and in the world and did not have to go to a church to find God. That isn't regression, that's progression. That's when you finally put it all together.

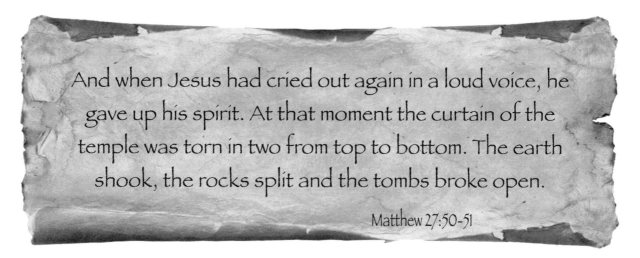

And when Jesus had cried out again in a loud voice, he gave up his spirit. At that moment the curtain of the temple was torn in two from top to bottom. The earth shook, the rocks split and the tombs broke open.

Matthew 27:50-51

Allen, how does the concept of revolution apply to Jesus, considering the historical connotations and complexities associated with the term, and what unique perspectives does examining Jesus through this lens offer?

I see Jesus as being revolutionary if we qualify that term carefully because that term is very loaded. We come to that term on the other side of several modern revolutions, some bourgeois revolutions, some proletarian revolutions, and some revolutions that have gone down the tubes recently. We know a lot about revolution and have a lot of sensibilities about that that may not apply directly to Jesus. I would characterize it in this way: the ancient Israelite tradition held to an ideal that a group of people who are called together by God would be ruled directly by God. There would be, as far as we could see on the human level, a tribal quasi-anarchistic confederacy with the common understanding that God was really the person in charge. And that's a very radical concept. And it was basically too radical for just about anybody, even Israel, traditionally. But they struggled with it. Centuries later, Jesus comes along and is captured by this ideal, which by this time is atavistic. It's kind of the old-time religion–that God wants to dwell in the midst of the people, wants to save the people from their problems, many of which they've caused themselves. Like we do. Most of our problems are problems that God would intervene directly to do that.

One of the problems was that Israel was a national dissolution whose ancestral land holdings were no longer theirs. They were no longer in control of their own political autonomy. Some of their people no longer live in the land. They've been dispersed. So the nation had been fractured. Well, if the blessing of God was contingent upon the health of the body politic, which is how Israel understood itself, what were you going to do? How were those people going to be brought back together? How were you going to undo the damage that history had done, or that people had done in history?

In ancient Israelite tradition, sin wasn't a purely personal affair. A nation could fall under the burden of sin. And sin had some concrete ramifications. Maybe the most influential philosophy of history in ancient Israel, was that Israel had come on hard times in part because of disobedience. It had failed as a nation to live up to the great responsibility that God had given it. It's a sin. Even if people weren't personally involved in that failure, that failure was their failure. And so that sin had to be lifted. That sin had to be forgiven. And in the ministry of Jesus and the activity of God, people could see that God had indeed forgiven them. That the curse was being lifted. The heavy burden of taxation, police brutality, and basic indignity. Want, poverty, hunger. These very concrete and painful ramifications of sin were all being addressed. They were all being challenged, they were being rolled back in the ministry of Jesus. People could see that God was really forgiving Israel, giving Israel another chance in the resurrection of Jesus. And even in his ministry, people could see that the limitations of their existence, and really of all human existence, were qualified, if not nullified, in what Jesus was doing, including death. And if there were any question about that, then the resurrection answers that question. So I would see him as a radical in view of the radical tradition.

Huston, how do you perceive the term "radical" in relation to Jesus' teachings?

Radical is a bad word in certain sectors. I happen to live in Berkeley, and radical is a good word in Berkeley. And the best of the Jesus scholars pick up on that. There's a world class Jewish scholar who teaches in my university, University of California. He spent two years learning Greek in order to understand Jesus better. And his book, it's one of the best written, and it's by a Jew, Is Jesus A Radical Jew. And that's the whole thesis. He was Jewish. But he was a Jewish radical and the radicalism consists precisely in not letting social, conventional guidelines like "You do not eat with the Samaritans," guide you. Guidelines that divided people and the absolute nonchalance, you might say, which he just wiped those all away and came down to the real thing - your one on one relationship to your neighbor. Do you give your neighbor the same standing in your desires, hopes, efforts, as you do your own interests. That's why it was radical. I am persuaded and convinced that the more we understand his message of love, what he was trying to get at, it is indeed the case that we just can't imagine virtue and compassion in these proportions.

Allen, how does your faith in Jesus influence your hope for achieving justice and equity, especially in challenging times?

I have a faith commitment that in a way is informed by certain political considerations. If you're interested in justice or dignity of people in an age like this that's a hard rule to hoe. The odds against realizing some kind of justice or equity or decency for common people is very difficult. If you want to struggle for that, you really have to believe in a miracle of some kind. You need that. That's what grabs me. I believe it. He beat it. Then it can be beaten. And that God has some kind of investment in that.

"Christ Blessing the Children," 1652-53, Nicolas Maes. This painting depicts Jesus blessing the little children, as described in the Gospel of Matthew (Chapter 19, verses 13-15), symbolizing Jesus' love for innocence and his teaching that the kingdom of God belongs to those who are like children.

"The Transfiguration," 1516-1520, Raffaello Sanzio. This painting depicts the moment of Jesus' transfiguration on Mount Tabor, as described in the Gospel of Matthew (Chapter 17, verses 1-9), symbolizing the revelation of Jesus' divine glory to Peter, James, and John and affirming his identity as the Son of God.

Richard, you've expressed that Jesus embodied a radical departure from conventional beliefs by encouraging individuals to trust their own experiences rather than conforming to societal expectations of perfection. Could you explain what you mean by that?

Jesus was a man born out of due time, that not only did he trust his own experience, but he gave other people the permission to share and to trust and to live out of their own experience. I'm convinced that's really what it means to carry the cross, to carry the burden of your own experience, even if it might be wrong. That's the cross. Because you're never sure that you're right. And that's why it's called faith. That you're not sure you're right, and yet I know that I am who I am who I am, and this is what I've gone through, and I've got to now carry this. The mystery of who I am.

One learns one's mystery at the price of one's innocence. And I think Jesus was willing to let go of his own false innocence about people needing to be perfect, or even he needing to be perfect. He never needs to present an image of himself as right or perfect. It's just, this is what I know. This is what I have to stand for, because this is what I've experienced. That is a categorically different way of teaching. And it really has not been appreciated in most of history. Which has, I think, castrated most human beings. Because most human beings are not academics, they're not educated. All most of us has is our own experience. And so this is a great liberation that we finally have a God figure who says that we can trust our own experience. And that we will be judged before God on that. Wherever it led us. And are we willing to pay the price for where it leads us.

When Jesus takes up the cross, I think he is saying, I am willing to bear the burden of my own reality, wherever it leads me. Never sure that it's right. That's why it's called faith. And why faith is so rare. And why Jesus said when the Son of Man returns, will he find any faith on earth? I think Jesus really had doubts. Because religion is common. It's on every street corner. Faith is very rare. Jesus came to teach faith.

Reflections

I learned in filmmaking that while the final work I created rarely matched my initial vision, it was always exactly what it was meant to be. The book is a different process and carries with it a clear benefit. I do not have to concern myself with forcing a narrative into a predetermined time slot. All of those pieces of wisdom that were on the cutting room floor can be considered as long as I don't run out of paper. With so much more content to work with and twenty-five additional years of life experience, I had expected to develop many new opinions and discover different themes and arcs in the story. I'm happy to say that didn't happen.

In creating the film, the key messages and insights became woven into my spiritual DNA. They became an integral part of who I am. While some nuances to the overall theme are evident, all of the key messages remain firmly intact. This is due in no small part to the collective wisdom of the three great thinkers I was able to include in the project and their rare ability to impart their gifts on those fortunate enough to sit in front of them and ask the right questions. But I would argue it was also because Jesus' message is timeless, clear, and simple, albeit decidedly difficult to realize. As T.S. Eliot so wisely put it, "We shall not cease from exploration, and the end of all our exploring will be to arrive where we started and know the place for the first time." This encapsulates the journey of understanding, where we delve deeply only to find profound truths that bring us back to the essence of what we have always known or have been fortunate enough to learn.

This is a summary, some restated and expanded on, from my reflections of the most impactful and lasting teachings that have, and I believe will continue to guide me.

It was a Movement

I interpret Jesus' journey into the desert as a profoundly symbolic metaphor, encapsulating a deeply authentic experience. His immediate transition from baptism by John the Baptist to his

> Jesus came from Nazareth in Galilee and was baptized by John in the Jordan. Just as Jesus was coming up out of the water, he saw heaven being torn open and the Spirit descending on him like a dove...At once the Spirit sent him out into the wilderness, and he was in the wilderness forty days, being tempted by Satan. He was with the wild animals, and angels attended him."
>
> (Mark 1:9-13)

solitary retreat into the Judean Desert, as the Gospel of Mark recounts, signified a pivotal shift—from a public declaration of his mission to a period of intense personal and spiritual strengthening.

Jesus journey highlights the critical role of solitude and testing in preparing for the monumental tasks ahead. And it underscores the necessity of inner strength and resilience, which are essential for initiating and sustaining the powerful movement he is to lead.

"Christ in the Wilderness," 1515-1520, Moretto da Brescia. This painting portrays Jesus in the wilderness, contemplating during his forty days of fasting and temptation, echoing the biblical account in Matthew 4:1-11. It symbolizes the spiritual preparation and resilience of Jesus before beginning his public ministry, emphasizing themes of faith, endurance, and triumph over temptation.

challenging existing societal norms and creating friction with both the Romans and the temple cult. By "hanging out at the bar," as Allen would phrase it, with marginalized groups—such as the poor, tax collectors, and women—Jesus broke significant social barriers, advocating for a society based on compassion rather than status. He frequently addresses the issue of wealth, highlighting its potential to corrupt and distract from spiritual growth. In this way, the movement is not only about spiritual enlightenment but also about demonstrating how spiritual truths can and should manifest in social justice, economic equity, and communal support. This dual focus on spiritual renewal and socio-economic reform makes his ministry a powerful, transformative movement that encountered resistance but also changed the course of history.

His words cut to the core

Jesus' words were deeply impactful, striking at the very heart or essence of the person or issue they addressed. They were so powerful that they elicited a strong emotional response, perhaps causing someone to rethink their beliefs, feel deeply understood, or be sharply criticized. His use of metaphor and parable is a defining aspect of his teaching style, serving both to communicate deep spiritual insights and to manage the social and political implications of his message. This approach allows him to convey profound, often uncomfortable truths and inherently radical ideas in a manner less likely to attract immediate backlash from the authorities who also had competing objectives with each other.

Parables were Jesus' most effective rhetorical tool and, at times, subtle weapon. These short stories used common scenes from everyday life to illustrate moral and spiritual lessons. Parables like the Good Samaritan or the Prodigal Son were simple on the surface but packed with layers of meaning, allowing listeners to draw various insights depending on their own spiritual openness and perspective. Parables require listeners to think deeply and interpret the meaning for themselves. As Huston Smith points out, "Jesus didn't put the emphasis on telling people what to do. The emphasis was putting it up to the listener." This method encourages personal reflection and allows the message to resonate on a deeper level, facilitating a more profound transformation than straightforward directives might achieve.

His skillful use of metaphors, which animated his parables, makes complex spiritual truths understandable to a broad audience, many of whom were not literate or educated in formal religious law. These storytelling methods are engaging and memorable, helping the teachings to be shared and retold effectively. By cloaking his messages in everyday language and scenarios, Jesus is able to discuss the principles of the Kingdom of God without directly antagonizing the Roman authorities or the temple priests—at least early in the movement. This is crucial in a time and place where direct criticism of the status quo could lead to severe consequences.

Allen's point bears repeating: "Jesus is in a highly charged, politically problematic, dangerous situation. So he's not going to lay his cards on the table all the time. And he's going to say things

"The Taking of Christ," 1602, Caravaggio. This painting vividly depicts the dramatic moment when Roman soldiers, guided by Judas betrayal with a kiss, come to arrest Jesus in the Garden of Gethsemane, as recounted in Mark 14:43-52. It captures the tense interaction between Jesus and his captors.

and wink. He knows what he's talking about. The people know what he's talking about. He knows they know. They know he knows. So there's a lot of communications going on there that's not being spoken. There's a lot of things going on between the lines."

Metaphor and parable also act as a filter; those who are genuinely interested and spiritually attuned ponder and understand the deeper meanings, while those who are dismissive or hostile might overlook or not recognize the subversive elements of the teachings.

The metaphor of metaphors

Matthew 7:14, as I described earlier, is the metaphor that resonates most deeply with me. A road that is not easy to navigate, leading to a gate that is supremely difficult to pass through, symbolizes a very difficult proposition. A journey like this requires a level of persistence that can only be derived from great faith. It is uncanny how often I see 7:14 on my watch, phone, and clock. The frequency defies coincidence. I believe it is a not-so-subtle reminder that I will ultimately fall short. Yet, it also underscores my obligation to myself and those around to keep pushing forward.

Unsurprisingly, the most potent of metaphors I take away from the Gospel of Matthew leads to the latter of the two Great Commandments: "Love your neighbor as yourself," (Matthew 22:37-40). No matter how complex the theological discussions that swirl in my head, this fundamental message has the power to cut through the fog. And like many of us, I find myself instinctively grasping for a more complex theological doctrine to lose myself in as a convenient escape and a form of "plausible deniability" if you will.

The redefining of true family

Jesus' teachings very often challenged traditional Jewish values, including the prioritization of familial ties. He proposed a redefinition of family based on spiritual kinship rather than just blood relations. These teachings were revolutionary and remain a challenge for those conditioned to believe that "blood is thicker than water." This philosophy can often keep someone trapped in environments that can be stifling, toxic, and even dangerous. This redefining is liberating for those who, through conditioning and guilt, often find the traditional familial construct impossible to escape. It was not a teaching I had heard in the eight years I attended church and something that made it easier to move on from such an environment.

This message is evident in several of Jesus' statements and actions recorded in the Gospels. In one notable incident, when Jesus was told that his mother and brothers were waiting outside to speak with him, he responded in a way that was radical for his time, as recorded by Matthew.

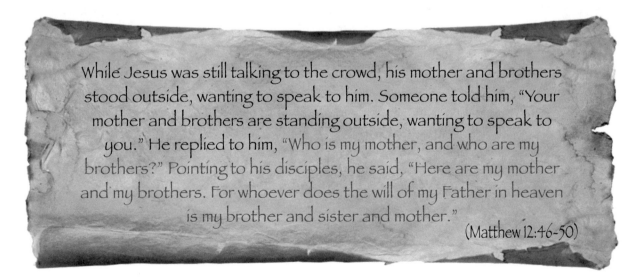

While Jesus was still talking to the crowd, his mother and brothers stood outside, wanting to speak to him. Someone told him, "Your mother and brothers are standing outside, wanting to speak to you." He replied to him, "Who is my mother, and who are my brothers?" Pointing to his disciples, he said, "Here are my mother and my brothers. For whoever does the will of my Father in heaven is my brother and sister and mother."

(Matthew 12:46-50)

This teaching redefines the concept of family in a spiritual context, emphasizing that true kinship is not solely a matter of blood relations but is forged through a shared faith of those who are, we might say, all "pulling in the same direction." Another striking example, as Allen pointed out, is Jesus' response to a disciple who asked to return home to bury his father before following Jesus.

As Allen noted, "That's the last act of filial piety in any traditional society. "Forget him." He says. "Let the dead bury the dead." People marshal various excuses for why they can't get with the program, and He's got an answer for all of these. And those answers are all very unflattering, unsavory, and hard." It underscored the urgency and priority of the spiritual journey over traditional familial obligations, including burial rites.

The temple outburst

The Romans generally adopted a policy of religious tolerance towards the various cultures within their empire, allowing a wide range of religious practices as long as these did not threaten public order or challenge Roman authority. Initially, Jesus did not seem to be a significant concern for the Romans. His teachings were primarily spiritual and moral, posing no direct challenge to Roman rule. However, the Jewish temple authorities, who maintained a delicate balance of cooperation with Roman rulers, perceived Jesus as a threat to their power. His challenges to their authority, criticisms of their practices, and his large and growing following made them nervous. They were concerned that his actions could provoke unrest, which would bring down the heavy hand of Roman intervention in Jewish affairs.

His cleansing of the temple, where he overturned the tables of the money changers, was the most significant public act of defiance against the commercial exploitation within religious practices. Given this backdrop, it was relatively straightforward for the temple authorities to frame Jesus'

actions and teachings as a potential threat to Roman rule. As Allen stated, "It is a prelude then to Jesus arrest. And the narrative implication is that Jesus called attention to Himself, and this is the engine that drove the temple establishment to finally come against him." By also presenting Jesus as claiming to be "King of the Jews," they could argue that he was establishing a basis for political rebellion, thus leveraging Roman concerns about security and governance to achieve their ends. Their portrayal of his movement as a threat to public order and imperial authority made it easier for the temple authorities to secure Roman intervention against him.

"Crucifixion (Detail Isenheim Altarpiece)," 1512-1516, Matthias Grünewald. This painting details the crucifixion of Jesus Christ, prominently displaying the INRI inscription and emphasizing his title as "King of the Jews."

This strategic portrayal ultimately led to Jesus' crucifixion, a method of execution typically reserved for slaves, insurgents, and those deemed "enemies of the state." It's no coincidence that the plaque affixed to the top of the cross that we see in many artworks was inscribed "INRI," which represents the initials of the Latin inscription "Iesus Nazarenus, Rex Iudaeorum," which translates to "Jesus of Nazareth, King of the Jews."

The Disciples

The disciples of Jesus sometimes appeared to struggle with fully embracing his teachings or exerting sufficient effort to follow him throughout his ministry. This tendency is poignantly illustrated during a crucial moment in his mission when, despite the significance of the circumstances, they succumbed to sleep. This incident occurred in the Garden of Gethsemane, just before Jesus' arrest, highlighting a critical lapse in vigilance and support at a time when he sought solidarity. This episode is detailed in the Gospel of Matthew 26:40, where Jesus finds his disciples asleep after asking them to stay awake and pray, underscoring the human frailties even among those closest to him.

And yet, after his death, they continued to spread his teachings and lead the movement he had begun, even as it increasingly came to be seen as a threat by both Roman authorities and Jewish religious leaders. This placed them in considerable danger. The historical accounts of the disciples' fates often mix historical tradition with legend. However, a common theme is that many of the disciples faced persecution and martyrdom.

- Peter was crucified in Rome under Emperor Nero's reign, around AD 64. It is said he requested to be crucified upside down, feeling unworthy to die in the same manner as Jesus.

- James is described in the Acts of the Apostles (Acts 12:1-2) as being executed by sword on the order of King Herod Agrippa I around AD 44.

- Paul, though not one of the original twelve disciples, was a crucial figure in early Christianity. He was arrested and, according to tradition, beheaded in Rome around AD 64-65, during the persecutions under Nero.

- Thomas traveled to India to spread the Christian faith, where he was eventually martyred, allegedly pierced by spears. Andrew is said to have been crucified in Greece on an X-shaped cross, now commonly referred to as "Saint Andrew's Cross."

- Various traditions suggest that other apostles also met martyrdom, though details often vary. For instance, Bartholomew is believed to have been flayed alive and then beheaded, and Matthew is thought to have been killed by the sword in Ethiopia.

"Crucifixion of Saint Peter," 1600, Caravaggio. This painting depicts Saint Peter being crucified upside down, reflecting his humility and unworthiness to die in the same manner as Jesus Christ. It relates to biblical themes found in John 21:18-19, where Jesus predicts Peter's martyrdom and emphasizes the sacrifice and devotion to faith exemplified in Peter's life.

How many of us would willingly succumb to such fates? The willingness of the disciples to face these kinds of deaths rather than renounce their faith is a powerful testament to the transformative impact of Jesus' message, inspiring generations of believers.

The humanity of Jesus

The historical existence of Jesus is widely supported by a combination of religious scriptures, non-Christian historical records, and scholarly consensus. And that is what continues to have the greatest pull on me—the humanity of Jesus. This is what inspired me to make the film. Was he really "a man of the people," as Allen describes him? Divine and human? As Father Rohr pointed out, "The most common word Jesus uses for himself, 79 times in fact, by far more than any other term, is this strange term that we've translated as 'Son of Man.' It really means 'Son of a human being,' one of you, every man. He's always calling himself 'Every Man.' The quintessential

"Christ and the Samaritan Woman," 1520-1530, Vincenzo Catena. This painting depicts Jesus Christ in conversation with the Samaritan woman at the well, emphasizing his humanity through compassionate interaction and profound spiritual teachings, as recounted in John 4:1-42. It underscores Christ's ability to bridge societal divides and offer divine grace to all, regardless of background or status.

human being. 'I'm what it means to be human. Just look at me and trust it.' This is what a real mensch, a real human being, would look like at its best."

Jesus words to his disciples are always, follow me, not worship me. As Father Rohr observes, "Most Christian services are preoccupied with worshiping Jesus. He's saying, follow me. Do what I'm doing. Come and live the way I'm living. A simple life in this world. A shared life in this world. A non violent life. A compassionate life.

The depth of faith required to live out this message is immense, both individually and collectively. Even Jesus, in a moment of vulnerability, questioned if his teachings would endure.

Yet, in this uncertainty lies hope. The very act of questioning signals the enduring relevance of his message. It calls us to rise, to embrace this faith with an intensity that defies doubt, ensuring that when the Son of Man does return, he will indeed find faith.

"...when the Son of Man comes, will he find faith on the earth?"

(Luke 18:8)

About the Artists

To follow, you will discover concise biographies of the 45 artists whose 77 combined works enrich the pages of this book. Each biography offers a glimpse into the lives of these extraordinary creators, whose artistic journeys are as captivating as the masterpieces they've produced. We invite you to explore their personal histories further, as their stories are woven with passion, struggle, and triumph, making them as compelling as the art itself.

By Luca Signorelli, (1501)

Fra Angelico, born Guido di Pietro (c. 1395 – 1455), was a masterful painter of the Early Italian Renaissance, primarily residing in Florence and the Dominican monastery of San Marco. Known for his ethereal style that incorporated a refined use of light and vibrant colors, Angelico marked a significant departure from the more rigid medieval styles, forging a path towards greater realism and emotional depth in religious art. His artworks mainly depicted religious scenes, deeply infused with Christian doctrine, often aiming to serve as visual sermons that enhance the viewer's spiritual reflection. His motivations were deeply rooted in his Christian faith, as a Dominican friar, his life and work were inextricably linked with the church, aiming to communicate religious truths and inspire devotion. Supported by patrons including the influential Medici family, much of his work remains in the monastery of San Marco in Florence, with significant pieces also featured in major museums around the world. His legacy is celebrated for its devout and transformative approach to Renaissance art.

By Daniele da Volterra (1545)

Michelangelo Buonarroti (1475–1564) was an iconic figure of the Italian Renaissance, primarily residing in Florence and Rome. His artistic style revolutionized Western art, characterized by dramatic expressions and powerful physicality, evident in both his sculptures and paintings. Michelangelo's subjects varied from religious to mythological, with a profound emphasis on human anatomy and emotion, reflecting deep humanist influences. His religious works, such as the Sistine Chapel ceiling and 'The Last Judgment,' were motivated by his personal faith and the desire to convey complex theological concepts through vivid imagery and dynamic composition. His relationship with Christianity was complex, intertwined with personal belief and the era's religious turmoil. Michelangelo had several patrons, most notably the Medici family and various popes, who commissioned his most famous works. Today, much of his art can be found in the Vatican Museums, the Accademia Gallery in Florence, and other prestigious institutions worldwide, maintaining his legacy as a master of the High Renaissance.

Self Portrait (1699)

Ludolf Bakhuizen (1630–1708), a notable figure in the Dutch Golden Age, spent much of his life in Amsterdam. He was renowned for his marine paintings, depicting detailed and dynamic seascapes that captured the turbulent beauty of the sea and the Dutch prowess in naval endeavors. His style was characterized by vigorous realism and skillful manipulation of light and shadow, which vividly brought to life the dramatic interactions between the sea and the sky. While Bakhuizen primarily focused on maritime subjects, any religious motifs in his work subtly reflected the Calvinist values of modesty and reverence towards God's creation. His relationship with Christianity, though not overtly prominent in his art, was embedded in the cultural and spiritual ethos of his time. Bakhuizen enjoyed the patronage of wealthy merchants and Dutch nobility, which helped secure his financial and artistic success. His masterpieces are predominantly housed in the Rijksmuseum in Amsterdam, ensuring his legacy as a master of maritime painting endures.

By unkown (1900)

Carl Heinrich Bloch (1834-1890) was a Danish painter who lived primarily in Copenhagen. He was a key figure in the 19th-century Danish art scene and is best known for his work in the Romantic style, which often depicted religious themes with profound emotional depth. Bloch painted a wide range of subjects, but he is most celebrated for his religious artwork, particularly his series of paintings illustrating the life of Christ. His motivations for these works were deeply rooted in his Christian faith, and he sought to capture the spiritual essence of biblical stories. Bloch's relationship with Christianity was both personal and professional, reflecting a deep reverence for the teachings of the Bible. He was commissioned by the King of Denmark, Christian IX, to create altarpieces for various churches, making the king one of his most significant patrons. Today, most of Bloch's artwork hangs in the Frederiksborg Palace in Denmark, where it continues to inspire viewers with its spiritual and artistic significance.

Anonymous (1585)

Hieronymus Bosch (c. 1450-1516) was a Dutch painter from 's-Hertogenbosch, a city from which he derived his name. Bosch is famed for his unique approach to painting, employing an intricate, symbolic style that has often been linked to the Northern Renaissance but defies complete classification. His works are characterized by fantastical imagery, complex narratives, and an exploration of moral and religious themes that reflect his deep Christian beliefs and the pessimistic spiritual environment of his time.Bosch's art predominantly features scenes from the Bible and vivid, allegorical representations of sin and redemption, which were motivated by his concerns over human morality and the fate of the soul after death. This thematic choice suggests a personal and contemplative relationship with Christianity, influenced by the religious turmoil of the late medieval period. Bosch did not work under the patronage of one specific individual but was commissioned by various nobles and religious institutions. Today, his most celebrated works, such as "The Garden of Earthly Delights," hang in prestigious museums such as the Museo del Prado in Madrid, embodying his profound and complex engagement with spiritual themes.

Paolo Uccello (1490's)

Giotto di Bondone (1267-1337), a revolutionary Italian painter from Florence, is celebrated as a pivotal figure in art, marking the transition from the Middle Ages to the Renaissance. He resided mainly in Florence but also worked extensively in Padua and Naples. Giotto's style broke away from the Byzantine tradition, introducing more naturalistic figures and emotionally resonant scenes. His frescoes, characterized by a remarkable depth of expression and innovation in human poses, had a monumental impact on Renaissance art. Giotto focused on religious subjects, motivated by his deep Christian faith and the ecclesiastical patronage that dominated the era. His artworks often depicted scenes from the life of Christ and the Virgin Mary, aiming to evoke empathy and moral contemplation from viewers. This approach reflected his personal devotion and the broader religious context of his time. Giotto was not tied to a single patron but was commissioned by various church authorities and wealthy laypersons. Most of his surviving masterpieces, like the frescoes in the Scrovegni Chapel in Padua and the Basilica of Saint Francis in Assisi, continue to be revered as foundational works of Western art.

By unkown

Duccio di Buoninsegna (c. 1255-1318) was a seminal Italian painter from Siena, whose work is a cornerstone of the Sienese School during the Late Middle Ages. Duccio is renowned for his refined use of color and his ability to convey emotional depth and spiritual solemnity, which marked a significant departure from the more rigid Byzantine style prevalent before his time. His painting primarily focused on religious themes, vividly depicting scenes from the life of Christ and the Virgin Mary. These works were deeply rooted in his Christian faith, aimed at inspiring reverence and piety among viewers.His relationship with Christianity was not merely professional but deeply personal, influencing his artistic expressions with profound spirituality and devotion. Duccio received commissions from religious institutions rather than a single patron, which was common in his era. Most of Duccio's works, including his famed Maestà altar piece, originally created for Siena Cathedral, now grace the walls of major museums such as the Museo dell'Opera del Duomo in Siena and the National Gallery in London, highlighting his enduring influence in religious and art history.

Philip Calderon (1881)

Briton Rivière (1840-1920) was a British artist known for his skillful animal paintings, residing for most of his life in London. Rivière's style blended academic art with naturalistic detail, making him a popular figure within the Royal Academy of Arts, where he was a frequent exhibitor. Although predominantly recognized for his depictions of animals, he occasionally ventured into historical and religious subjects, which were infused with the same realism and emotive quality seen in his animal works. His religious paintings, like "Daniel in the Lions' Den," sought to explore themes of faith and divine intervention, reflecting his interest in the dramatic and moral aspects of biblical stories. Rivière's relationship with Christianity, as seen through his artworks, was more exploratory and interpretative rather than devout, focusing on the human and moral dimensions of religious narratives. He did not rely on a single patron but was supported by a wide array of private collectors and public commissions. Today, Rivière's works are held in major UK galleries, including the Tate Britain and the Victoria and Albert Museum, showcasing his versatility and enduring appeal as an artist.

Ottavio Leoni (1621)

Caravaggio (1571-1610) was born Michelangelo Merisi in Milan, Italy, and died in Porto Ercole. He primarily lived and worked in Rome, where he revolutionized painting with his distinctive Baroque style characterized by intense chiaroscuro and dramatic realism. Caravaggio's subjects ranged widely from religious scenes to genre paintings, focusing on biblical figures and everyday life with equal intensity. His religious artworks often depicted biblical narratives with a raw and humanistic approach, aiming to bring spiritual themes closer to the viewer through vivid realism and emotional depth. His relationship with Christianity was complex; while he deeply explored religious themes, his personal life was often tumultuous, marked by controversy and even criminal behavior. Caravaggio had several patrons throughout his career, including wealthy collectors and church officials, who supported his innovative but controversial artistic vision. Today, much of his artwork hangs in prestigious museums and galleries worldwide, including the Vatican Museums and the Uffizi Gallery in Florence, reflecting his enduring influence on Western art.

Self Portrait (1510)

Vincenzo Catena (c. 1470-1531) was an Italian painter known for his work in Venice, where he lived and worked for most of his life. He painted primarily in the Venetian Renaissance style, characterized by rich colors, attention to detail, and a focus on light and atmosphere. Catena's subjects ranged widely from religious and mythological scenes to portraits and genre paintings, showcasing his versatility and technical skill. In his religious artworks, Catena aimed to convey spiritual narratives with a sense of grace and dignity, often depicting biblical figures and scenes with a humanistic touch that emphasized their emotional and moral aspects. His relationship with Christianity was devout, evident in his meticulous portrayal of religious themes that sought to inspire piety and reflection. Catena had various patrons, including prominent Venetian families and religious institutions, who commissioned works for private chapels and public display. Today, his artworks are primarily found in museums such as the National Gallery in London and the Louvre in Paris, reflecting his enduring legacy in Renaissance art.

Nicolas de Larmessin unkown

Cimabue (Cenni di Pepo), born around 1240 and died in 1302, was a pioneering figure in Italian art, heralded as one of the last great painters of the Byzantine style before the advent of the Renaissance. Operating primarily in Florence, he is known for transitioning away from the italo-Byzantine art forms, infusing greater naturalism into religious scenes. Cimabue's works largely encompass religious motifs, with his frescoes and panel paintings depicting scenes from the life of Christ and the Virgin Mary, aimed at narrating biblical stories with emotional depth and reverence. His engagement with Christianity was profound, as his artworks served to both educate and inspire devotion in a predominantly Christian audience. Unlike many of his contemporaries who worked under specific patrons, Cimabue was largely commissioned by the church, reflecting his integral role in the religious and artistic community. Most of his surviving works, such as the celebrated 'Santa Trinita Madonna' and 'Maestà of Santa Maria dei Servi,' are preserved in the Uffizi Gallery in Florence and the Basilica of San Francesco in Assisi, attracting admirers of medieval art.

Unkown (1845)

Thomas Cole (1801-1848) was an English-born painter who became one of the foremost figures in American art as the founder of the Hudson River School. Living and working primarily in New York, Cole is best known for his expansive landscapes that depict the American wilderness with a romantic and almost spiritual reverence. His painting style, characterized by meticulous detail and dramatic light, aimed to showcase the sublime beauty of nature and its divine creator, aligning with the broader transcendentalist movement of the time.Cole's subjects often included scenes that, while primarily naturalistic, carried strong moral and religious overtones, reflecting his personal views on the spiritual significance of nature. His religious artworks were motivated by a belief in nature as a manifestation of God, intended to elicit awe and moral reflection in the viewer. While Cole did not have a consistent patron, his works were highly sought after by art collectors and institutions. Today, most of his artwork hangs in major American museums like the Metropolitan Museum of Art in New York and the National Gallery of Art in Washington, D.C., highlighting his lasting influence on American landscape painting.

Nadar (1856-1858)

Gustave Doré (1832-1883) was a French artist and illustrator, renowned for his prolific work and impact on 19th-century visual culture. Doré lived most of his life in Paris, where he created vast and influential artworks in a dramatic and imaginative style. He was best known for his lavish illustrations that graced the pages of literary classics like Dante's "Divine Comedy," Cervantes' "Don Quixote," and the Bible. His style, rich in detail and epic in scope, brought dramatic and emotional depth to these narratives, appealing broadly to the Victorian sensibilities of his time.Doré's religious illustrations were motivated by a desire to visualize the grandeur and depth of biblical stories, reflecting his personal engagement with Christian themes. His relationship with Christianity was both artistic and personal, using his art to explore and express complex spiritual themes. Though not tied to a single patron, his works were commissioned by a wide array of publishers and institutions. Today, Doré's artworks are held in major museums worldwide, including the Musée d'Orsay in Paris and the British Museum in London, attesting to his enduring legacy in both art and illustration.

Self Portrait (1638)

Artemisia Gentileschi (1593-1653) was a groundbreaking Italian Baroque painter who spent much of her career in Florence, Rome, and Naples, with notable periods in London. As one of the first women to achieve recognition in the art world, Gentileschi is celebrated for her vivid depictions of dramatic and powerful female figures, often from biblical and mythological narratives. Her style is marked by intense realism, strong chiaroscuro, and dynamic compositions, which reflect the influence of Caravaggio, whom she admired.Gentileschi's religious paintings, including her famous interpretations of Judith Slaying Holofernes, were driven by personal experience and a nuanced perspective on biblical women's strength and resilience. These works reveal her complex relationship with Christianity—where faith intersects with a profound scrutiny of its narratives through a distinctly female lens. While Gentileschi did not have one consistent patron, she received commissions from various influential figures and institutions. Today, her art is prominently displayed in major museums such as the Uffizi Gallery in Florence and the National Gallery in London, underscoring her status as a key figure in Baroque art.

Thomas Hicks (1839)

Edward Hicks (1780-1849) was an American folk painter and Quaker minister who spent his entire life in and around Bucks County, Pennsylvania. Hicks is best known for his distinctive style of naive art, primarily focusing on the themes of peace and biblical prophecy, which resonated deeply with his Quaker beliefs. His most celebrated series of paintings, "The Peaceable Kingdom," illustrates Isaiah's biblical prophecy of a harmonious world where predators and prey lie together in peace, reflecting Hicks' aspirations for a utopian society and his pacifist religious convictions. His works were motivated by his desire to spread the Quaker ideals of simplicity, integrity, and peace, using his art as a form of spiritual and moral teaching. Hicks did not have a traditional patron; instead, he supported himself through his craft, painting ornamental designs on coaches and household items when not producing fine art. Today, most of Edward Hicks' artwork hangs in American museums such as the National Gallery of Art in Washington, D.C., and the Philadelphia Museum of Art, celebrating his unique contribution to American folk art and religious painting.

Self Portrait (1855)

Heinrich Hofmann (1824-1911) was a German painter renowned for his profound contributions to Christian art, spending much of his life in Dresden. Hofmann specialized in religious scenes, deeply influenced by the Nazarene movement, which sought to revive the spirituality and simplicity of medieval art in contrast to the prevailing academic styles of his time. His paintings, characterized by a gentle realism and soft, harmonious colors, primarily depicted the life of Jesus Christ, aiming to inspire piety and devotion among viewers. Hofmann's religious works were driven by his personal Christian faith and a desire to visually communicate biblical stories with emotional depth and accessible clarity. He did not rely on a single patron but received commissions from various churches and religious institutions throughout Germany. Today, Hofmann's most revered pieces, such as "Christ in the Temple" and "Christ and the Rich Young Ruler," are displayed in prominent collections including the Riverside Church in New York and the Städel Museum in Frankfurt, demonstrating his enduring appeal and influence in religious art.

Self Portrait (1867)

William Holman Hunt (1827-1910) was a British painter, one of the founding members of the Pre-Raphaelite Brotherhood, residing primarily in London but also spending significant periods in the Middle East. Hunt's style is characterized by its vivid color, intricate detail, and commitment to naturalism, challenging the conventions of Victorian art. He focused on both religious and secular themes, with his religious works deeply influenced by his devout Christian beliefs and his travels in Palestine. These pieces, such as "The Light of the World" and "The Scapegoat," aim to visually sermonize, using detailed symbolism to explore themes of sin and redemption. Hunt's relationship with Christianity was intensely personal and reflected in his meticulous approach to biblical accuracy and spiritual symbolism. He did not have a consistent patron but was supported by a wide circle of Pre-Raphaelite enthusiasts and collectors. Most of his artwork is housed in major British institutions like the Tate Britain and the Manchester Art Gallery, ensuring his legacy as a key figure in the Pre-Raphaelite movement and a pioneer of religious painting.

Self Portrait (1650)

Jacob Jordaens (1593-1678) was a prominent Flemish painter from Antwerp, a key figure in the Baroque movement and one of the leading artists in 17th century Flanders after Rubens and Van Dyck. Jordaens' style is recognized for its vibrant energy, robust figures, and dynamic compositions, largely influenced by his predecessor Peter Paul Rubens. He painted a wide range of subjects, including mythological, historical, and allegorical scenes, but he is particularly noted for his religious and genre paintings. Jordaens' religious works were deeply rooted in his Reformed Protestant faith, often depicting biblical narratives with a focus on moral messages and human virtues, tailored to resonate with the Calvinist doctrines prevalent in his community.Unlike many artists of his time, Jordaens did not work with a single patron but received commissions from a diverse clientele, including town councils, religious groups, and private individuals. Today, much of his artwork hangs in prestigious museums around the world, including the Royal Museum of Fine Arts in Antwerp and the Hermitage Museum in St. Petersburg, showcasing his lasting influence on the Baroque art scene.

Josef Anton Trčka (1914)

Gustav Klimt (1862-1918) was an Austrian painter who spent much of his life in Vienna, becoming a central figure in the Art Nouveau movement. Klimt's style is famed for its sensuality, ornate gold leafing, and complex symbolic patterns, making him a leading member of the Vienna Secession movement. His subjects ranged from portraits to allegorical themes, and although not predominantly religious, his works often touched on existential themes and the human condition, embodying a secular spirituality. Klimt's approach to these themes was influenced by his personal philosophy rather than traditional Christian narratives, focusing on the beauty and mystery of life and nature. Klimt did not rely on a single patron, instead garnering support from a variety of influential art patrons and cultural leaders in Vienna. His most famous works, like "The Kiss" and "Portrait of Adele Bloch-Bauer I," hang in prestigious venues such as the Belvedere Museum in Vienna, reflecting his profound impact on modern art and his exploration of symbolism that extends beyond conventional religious motifs.

Self Portrait (1867)

Ivan Kramskoy (1837-1887) was a Russian painter and intellectual leader among the 19th-century Russian art community, primarily residing in St. Petersburg. Kramskoy was a principal member of the Peredvizhniki (Wanderers), a group advocating for realism and social commentary in art. His style is noted for its thoughtful depiction of character and mood, focusing on portraits, historical figures, and social themes. While not extensively religious, his subjects occasionally touched on spiritual themes, reflecting a complex, often critical view of organized religion, which mirrored his personal skepticism towards the institutional church in Russia. Kramskoy's nuanced approach to religious themes sought to explore the deeper, personal experiences of faith and morality rather than conventional biblical representations. He received commissions from a range of patrons, including fellow intellectuals and members of the Russian aristocracy. Today, Kramskoy's works are predominantly displayed in major Russian museums, such as the Tretyakov Gallery in Moscow and the Russian Museum in St. Petersburg, highlighting his significant influence on Russian art and thought.

Sante Pacini (1769)

Andrea Mantegna (1431-1506) was an Italian Renaissance painter who spent much of his career in Mantua, where he served as a court artist for the Gonzaga family. Renowned for his mastery of perspective and detailed, sculptural figures, Mantegna's style is a hallmark of the early Renaissance, blending classical motifs with innovative compositions. His subjects were diverse, encompassing religious scenes, classical myths, and portraits, with religious paintings predominating. Mantegna's religious works, deeply influenced by his devout Christian faith, often featured dramatic narratives from the Bible, aimed at evoking spiritual reflection and devotion. His motivations for such artworks were rooted in both his personal piety and the desire to enhance religious worship through visually compelling narratives. As the principal artist for the Gonzaga court, he enjoyed consistent patronage, which allowed him significant artistic freedom. Today, most of Mantegna's artwork hangs in major museums, including the Louvre in Paris and the Uffizi Gallery in Florence, securing his legacy as one of the seminal figures of the Italian Renaissance.

Self Portrait (1865)

Nicolas Maes (1634-1693) was a Dutch painter from Dordrecht who later moved to Amsterdam, becoming one of Rembrandt's most talented pupils and a notable figure of the Dutch Golden Age. Maes is best known for his genre scenes and portraits, but he also created a significant number of religious works. His painting style evolved from the detailed and dramatic chiaroscuro typical of Rembrandt's influence to a brighter, more colorful palette in his later years. His religious paintings often focused on intimate, contemplative moments, aiming to capture the quiet piety and personal devotion characteristic of Dutch Reformed Protestantism. Maes' motivations for his religious artworks were rooted in his personal faith and the cultural milieu of the 17th-century Netherlands, which valued modesty and moral introspection. He did not have a single patron but was supported by the commissions from the wealthy merchant class in Amsterdam. Today, much of his work, including his acclaimed religious and domestic scenes, hangs in major museums such as the Rijksmuseum in Amsterdam and the National Gallery in London, where his legacy as a master of genre and portrait painting endures.

MASACCIO. DA S. GIOVANNI. PITTORE.
M A S A C C I O.

Nicolas de Larmessin (1682)

Tommaso di Ser Giovanni di Simone, known as Masaccio (1401-1428), was a pioneering Italian painter from the early Renaissance, primarily active in Florence. His brief but impactful career is noted for introducing a more naturalistic and emotive style to religious art, which was a significant departure from the ornate Gothic norms. Masaccio's mastery of perspective and chiaroscuro added dramatic realism to his biblical scenes, effectively conveying the human drama and divine significance of Christian stories. His frescoes, such as those in the Brancacci Chapel, are celebrated for their depth and innovation, portraying subjects with a powerful sense of presence and spirituality. Masaccio's religious works were motivated by an earnest desire to depict Christian themes with authenticity and emotional impact, reflecting his own devout faith. While he did not have a single patron, he was commissioned by various influential figures of his time, including the powerful Medici family. Today, Masaccio's revolutionary artworks are primarily preserved in Florence, notably in the Santa Maria del Carmine and the Uffizi Gallery, marking his profound influence on the course of Western art.

Minya Diez-Dührkoop (1929)

Emil Nolde (1867-1956) was a German-Danish painter known for his vivid expressionist works, residing mainly in northern Germany near the Danish border. Nolde's style, characterized by intense color use and dynamic forms, played a significant role in the early 20th-century Expressionist movement. He painted a broad range of subjects, including landscapes, seascapes, urban scenes, and especially religious themes, infusing each with profound emotional force and spiritual intensity. His religious artworks, often depicting biblical scenes, were motivated by his complex relationship with Christianity, exploring themes of suffering, redemption, and the divine presence in a modern, turbulent world.Despite his complicated affiliation with the Nazi regime, which branded his work as "degenerate," Nolde continued to produce religious art that expressed both his personal faith and his existential struggles. He did not rely on a single patron but was supported by various art collectors and institutions throughout his career. Today, Nolde's works are featured in major museums worldwide, including the Emil Nolde Museum in Seebüll, Germany, which houses the largest collection of his art.

Hans Christian Henneberg (1865-1868)

Henrik Olrik (1830-1890) was a Danish painter and sculptor who spent much of his life in Copenhagen. He was a prominent figure in the Danish Golden Age of painting, a period marked by a focus on nationalism and romanticized historical themes. Olrik's style blended romanticism with a realistic portrayal of his subjects, which included portraits, historical figures, and religious scenes. His religious paintings were often inspired by his Lutheran faith, aiming to express spiritual themes with emotional depth and reverence. These works reflected his interest in both the human aspect and the divine intervention in biblical stories. Olrik's relationship with Christianity was deeply personal and influenced much of his artwork, serving as a spiritual exploration as well as artistic expression. He did not have a single patron but was commissioned by various institutions, including the Danish Royal Family. Today, most of Olrik's works are displayed in major Danish museums such as the Statens Museum for Kunst and the Hirschsprung Collection in Copenhagen, showcasing his contributions to 19th-century Danish art.

Self Portrait (1885)

Rebecca Orpen (1830-1923) was a British-Irish artist and miniaturist who lived much of her life at Ballynatray, Ireland, after marrying her cousin Edward Richard Townsend. Her work primarily in the Victorian style, Rebecca painted portraits and landscapes, capturing the genteel life of her social circle with delicate precision and rich detail. Though not extensively known for religious art, her works occasionally touched on religious themes, reflecting the typical Victorian engagement with Christian subjects through a personal, introspective lens. Orpen's relationship with Christianity, like many of her contemporaries, was shaped by the cultural norms of her time, which saw religion as both a moral authority and a source of artistic inspiration. She did not have a specific patron; instead, her position in society provided her the platform and audience for her art. Today, much of Rebecca Orpen's artwork remains in private collections, with some pieces held by historical homes and local Irish museums, reflecting her status as a skilled but relatively underrecognized figure in 19th-century art.

Alphonse Legros (1877)

Sir Edward John Poynter (1836-1919) was a prominent British painter and a key figure in the academic art scene of the late 19th century. Poynter lived and worked mainly in London, where he also served as the President of the Royal Academy of Arts. His style, deeply rooted in the academic tradition, was characterized by classical themes, precision in detail, and a vibrant portrayal of both mythological and biblical subjects. His religious artworks, including notable pieces like "Israel in Egypt," reflect a fascination with the grandeur and drama of biblical narratives, executed with meticulous historical accuracy.Poynter's relationship with Christianity, though not overtly devout in a personal sense, was more an academic and aesthetic exploration of its themes and histories. He did not rely on a single patron, but his positions and reputation helped secure numerous commissions from both private individuals and public institutions. Today, much of his work is displayed in major galleries such as the Tate Britain and the Victoria and Albert Museum, showcasing his mastery in depicting classical dignity and splendor.

Giorgio Vasari (1767)

Barna da Siena, also known as Bernardo di Biagio, was an Italian painter active from about 1330 until his untimely death in 1350. Operating mainly in Siena, he was a prominent figure in the Sienese School, which was known for its detailed and decorative style, closely aligned with the Gothic art prevalent during the Middle Ages. Barna da Siena's works predominantly featured religious subjects, capturing biblical scenes with intense emotional expression and intricate iconography, aimed at fostering a deeper spiritual reflection among viewers. His paintings often mirrored the devout Christian ethos of Siena, characterized by a strong emphasis on morality and piety. Barna's artistic motivations were deeply intertwined with his Christian faith, which sought to express and communicate religious narratives effectively and devoutly. While there is little information about specific patrons, it is likely that he was commissioned by local churches and religious institutions. Most of his remaining artwork, which includes frescoes in the Collegiata di San Gimignano, reflects his commitment to depicting religious themes with earnestness and fervor.

Self Portrait (1602)

Guido Reni (1575-1642) was an influential Italian painter of the Baroque period, primarily based in Bologna and later in Rome. Reni was renowned for his graceful and refined style, characterized by soft, luminous colors and an ethereal quality that distinguished him from his contemporaries. His subjects were predominantly religious, reflecting his deep Christian faith and the Catholic Reformation's emphasis on art as a vehicle for spiritual renewal. Reni's religious paintings, such as "The Assumption of the Virgin" and "Saint Joseph with the Infant Jesus," aimed to evoke the divine through beauty and emotional resonance, intended to inspire piety and devotion in viewers. Reni's relationship with Christianity was profoundly personal, influencing not only his thematic choices but also his artistic expression, which sought to portray religious figures with both sanctity and humanity. He enjoyed the patronage of wealthy cardinals and other ecclesiastical figures, which allowed him a considerable degree of artistic freedom. Today, much of Guido Reni's work is displayed in major museums across Europe, including the Louvre in Paris and the Prado in Madrid, celebrating his legacy as a master of Baroque painting.

Self Portrait (1623)

Peter Paul Rubens (1577-1640) was a Flemish Baroque painter, born in Siegen, Germany, but primarily based in Antwerp, Belgium. Rubens is celebrated for his exuberant and dramatic style, characterized by vibrant color, movement, and sensuality. His subjects spanned historical, mythological, and religious themes, with the latter deeply influenced by the Counter-Reformation's call for art that communicated Catholic values emotively and vividly. Rubens' religious works, such as "The Elevation of the Cross" and "The Descent from the Cross," aimed to inspire faith and devotion through their dynamic composition and emotional depth.His relationship with Christianity was not only personal but also professional, as he created numerous altarpieces and religious paintings that align with Catholic doctrine. Rubens enjoyed the patronage of various European monarchs and church leaders, which provided him with considerable resources and freedom in his artistic endeavors. Today, Rubens' masterpieces are displayed in major museums worldwide, including the Louvre in Paris and the Prado in Madrid, underscoring his stature as one of the foremost painters of the Baroque period.

Self Portrait (1506)

Raffaello Sanzio, known as Raphael (1483-1520), was an Italian painter and architect, a master of the High Renaissance, born in Urbino and primarily active in Florence and Rome. Raphael is renowned for his perfect and graceful style, which harmonized the best of his contemporaries' insights into balance, composition, and form. His subject matter was diverse, encompassing portraits, mythological scenes, and extensive religious compositions. His religious works, such as "The School of Athens" and "The Transfiguration," are celebrated for their clarity of form and serene narrative, crafted to elevate the viewer's spiritual experience.Raphael's deep relationship with Christianity was reflected in his devout portrayal of biblical scenes, aiming to visually translate the teachings of the Church with elegance and emotional resonance. He enjoyed the patronage of the most influential figures of his time, including Pope Julius II and his successors, which allowed him an unparalleled opportunity to craft his art. Today, Raphael's works are pivotal highlights in major museums such as the Vatican Museums in Rome and the Louvre in Paris, attesting to his enduring legacy in the annals of art history.

Self Portrait (1838)

Ary Scheffer (1795-1858) was a Dutch-French painter who spent most of his career in Paris, becoming a prominent figure in the Romantic movement. His style is characterized by its emotive intensity and a focus on moral and spiritual themes. Scheffer painted a variety of subjects, including portraits, historical scenes, and particularly religious works. His religious paintings, such as "The Temptation of Christ" and "St. Augustine and Monica," often explored themes of redemption, suffering, and divine love, reflecting his deep engagement with Christian doctrine and his personal piety. Scheffer's relationship with Christianity was complex and personal, profoundly influencing his artistic motivations to convey spiritual and ethical messages. He was favored by leading figures of his time, including King Louis-Philippe of France, who became his major patron. Today, Ary Scheffer's artworks are displayed in several prestigious institutions, notably the Louvre in Paris and the Hermitage Museum in St. Petersburg, showcasing his legacy as a painter who adeptly merged romantic aesthetics with profound religious sentiment.

Arthur Hughes (Unknown)

William Bell Scott (1811-1890) was a Scottish painter and poet, primarily associated with the Pre-Raphaelite Brotherhood and based in Newcastle upon Tyne for much of his career. His style, while influenced by the detailed naturalism of the Pre-Raphaelites, often incorporated elements of the historical and mythical, showcasing a blend of romantic and realistic sensibilities. Scott painted a range of subjects including historical scenes, landscapes, and occasionally, religious themes. His religious works were motivated by a scholarly interest in biblical and medieval stories rather than devout spirituality, reflecting a Victorian fascination with gothic and religious symbolism.Scott's relationship with Christianity was more intellectual and aesthetic than devout, aligning with the broader cultural trends of his era that sought to explore historical and moral narratives through art. He did not have a single patron but was supported by various commissions and his position as a master of the Government School of Design in Newcastle. Today, his works can be found in key British collections, including the Tate Britain and the National Gallery of Scotland, highlighting his contributions to 19th-century British art.

Unknown

Ikarashi Shunmei (1892-1971) was a Japanese painter known for his Nihonga-style paintings, a genre that emphasizes traditional Japanese techniques and aesthetics. Based predominantly in Tokyo throughout his career, Shunmei specialized in landscapes and portraits that often incorporated elements of Japanese spirituality and mythology. While not primarily focused on overtly religious subjects, his works subtly reflected Shinto and Buddhist themes, portraying nature and human figures with a reverence that hints at the divine. Shunmei's approach to spirituality in art was less about organized religion and more about an intrinsic, almost pantheistic connection to the natural world, which aligns with traditional Japanese religious views. He did not have a specific patron but was supported by the broader cultural patronage of the arts in Japan, which valued the preservation and continuation of traditional styles. Today, Shunmei's works are held in several prestigious Japanese institutions, including the Tokyo National Museum and the Adachi Museum of Art, showcasing his mastery in blending modern sensibilities with ancient techniques.

Unknown (1856)

Émile Signol (1804-1892) was a French painter, a notable figure in the academic and neoclassical movements, spending the majority of his life in Paris. Signol's style was characterized by its precision, clear composition, and often, the use of religious and historical subjects that echoed the grandeur of earlier Renaissance works. His religious paintings, such as "The Martyrdom of Saint Stephen" and "Christ on the Mount of Olives," were motivated by a desire to convey the moral and spiritual lessons inherent in biblical stories, reflecting his devout Catholic faith. Signol's relationship with Christianity was deeply personal and influenced much of his artistic output, using his skills to express his spirituality and engage the viewer in religious contemplation. He enjoyed the patronage of the French state and various religious institutions, which commissioned many of his works. Today, Signol's paintings can be found in several major French museums, including the Louvre and the Musée d'Orsay, preserving his legacy as a master of neoclassical religious art.

Self Portrait (1885)

James Smetham (1821-1889) was an English painter and poet who spent most of his life in London. Smetham was associated with the Pre-Raphaelite Brotherhood, adopting their emphasis on detailed naturalism and vibrant color, though he developed a distinct style characterized by its emotional intensity and spiritual depth. His subjects varied from landscapes to literary themes, but he is particularly noted for his religious paintings. These works were deeply influenced by his devout Methodist faith, which sought to convey spiritual and moral messages through biblical scenes and allegorical subjects. Smetham's relationship with Christianity was central to his life and art, influencing both his subjects and his approach to painting. He did not have a single, consistent patron, instead supported by a network of friends and admirers within the artistic and religious communities. Most of Smetham's artwork remains relatively obscure, with several pieces held in private collections and a few in institutions like the Tate Britain, reflecting his modest but respected position in Victorian art circles.

Self Portrait (1595-1600)

Domenikos Theotokopoulos, known as El Greco (1541-1614), was a Greek painter who spent the latter part of his life in Toledo, Spain. El Greco is famed for his idiosyncratic style, characterized by elongated figures and vibrant, often surreal color palettes, which departed from the conventions of his Renaissance contemporaries to forge a unique blend of Byzantine traditions and Western painting techniques. His subjects primarily included religious themes, portraits, and occasional landscapes, with his religious artworks deeply motivated by his Orthodox Christian upbringing and later interactions with Catholic Spain. These paintings often reflect intense spiritual emotion and a mystic contemplation of divinity, aimed at evoking a profound religious experience. El Greco's relationship with Christianity was intense and personal, heavily influencing his artistic expression. He was commissioned by various church figures and institutions in Toledo, which allowed him some artistic liberty. Today, most of his artwork hangs in major museums worldwide, including the Prado Museum in Madrid and the Metropolitan Museum of Art in New York, showcasing his lasting impact on the art world.

Self Portrait (1865)

James Tissot (1836-1902) was a French painter who spent significant periods of his career in Paris and London. Tissot initially gained recognition for his depictions of fashionable society before undergoing a spiritual awakening in the late 1880s, which profoundly shifted his focus towards religious subjects. His style, characterized by meticulous detail and vibrant realism, was well-suited to his later biblical themes, which he pursued with zeal after a life-changing pilgrimage to the Holy Land. These religious works, such as "The Life of Christ," were motivated by his desire to visually translate the New Testament into accessible, emotionally resonant scenes that combined historical accuracy with contemporary insights. Tissot's relationship with Christianity was deeply personal and reflective, influencing not only the subjects he chose but also the way he portrayed them, aiming to bridge the gap between biblical times and modern viewers. He did not rely on a single patron but was supported by the sales of his paintings and prints. Today, much of his artwork, including his religious series, is held in public and private collections worldwide, with significant holdings in the Brooklyn Museum and the Musée d'Orsay.

Self Portrait (1655)

Gerard van Honthorst (1592-1656) was a Dutch painter, prominent in Utrecht and later in The Hague, known for his influence in the Dutch Golden Age and his significant contributions to the Caravaggisti style, marked by dramatic use of light and shadow. Honthorst was famed for his night scenes where light played a central role, earning him the nickname "Gherardo delle Notti." His subjects varied from genre scenes to portraits and religious themes, with his religious paintings deeply motivated by the Counter-Reformation's call for art that was emotionally compelling and instructive. These works often featured intense, dramatic illumination to highlight moments of divine intervention or moral decision, aiming to make biblical stories vivid and accessible. Honthorst's relationship with Christianity was both profound and pragmatic, helping to communicate the spiritual and ethical messages of his time. He enjoyed the patronage of both Protestant and Catholic clients, including royalty across Europe. Today, Honthorst's artworks are displayed in major museums worldwide, such as the Louvre in Paris and the National Gallery in London, showcasing his mastery of light and narrative.

Self Portrait (1878)

Vincent Willem van Gogh (1853-1890) was a Dutch post-impressionist painter who spent his career in the Netherlands and France, transforming the vibrancy and emotional depth of his works into a cornerstone of modern art. Van Gogh's style is notable for its bold, dramatic brush strokes and vivid color palette, exploring subjects from landscapes and night scenes to portraits and still lifes. His religious artworks, such as "The Good Samaritan" and "The Raising of Lazarus," were driven by his complex relationship with Christianity, initially shaped by his early desire to serve as a clergyman. These works reflect his ongoing spiritual struggles and his attempt to find solace and meaning through art. Van Gogh's deep personal faith evolved into a broader, more existential questioning, yet his works continued to engage with spiritual themes, seeking to convey his inner emotional landscape. Lacking a consistent patron, van Gogh was largely supported by his brother Theo. Today, his masterpieces hang in prestigious museums worldwide, including the Van Gogh Museum in Amsterdam and the Musée d'Orsay in Paris, attesting to his profound impact on the art world.

Self Portrait (1659)

Rembrandt van Rijn (1606-1669) was a Dutch master painter and etcher, one of the greatest visual artists in the history of art, and a pivotal figure in the Dutch Golden Age. Residing primarily in Amsterdam, Rembrandt's style evolved from the smooth, detailed realism of his early works to a more luminous and expressive technique in his later years. He painted a wide range of subjects, including portraits, landscapes, and historical and mythological scenes, but he is particularly noted for his religious works. These paintings, such as "The Return of the Prodigal Son" and "Christ in the Storm on the Sea of Galilee," reflect his deep Christian faith and his contemplation of the human condition, focusing on themes of repentance, grace, and divine mercy. Rembrandt's relationship with Christianity was personal and introspective, profoundly influencing his approach to biblical narratives. Although he received commissions from various patrons throughout his career, financial instability was a constant struggle. Today, Rembrandt's works are treasured in major museums worldwide, including the Rijksmuseum in Amsterdam and the Hermitage Museum in St. Petersburg, showcasing his unmatched skill in portraying the depths of human emotion and spirituality.

Self Portrait (1656)

Johannes Vermeer (1632-1675) was a Dutch Baroque painter who lived and worked in Delft, Netherlands, throughout his life. Known for his masterful use of light and color, Vermeer specialized in domestic interior scenes of middle-class life, which are marked by a profound sense of tranquility and meticulous detail. Though Vermeer's known works are few, about thirty-five paintings, they include a small number of religious subjects, such as "Christ in the House of Martha and Mary," which showcase his ability to infuse everyday scenes with a sense of spiritual dignity and quiet reverence. Vermeer's religious artworks, though not the primary focus of his oeuvre, reflect a Calvinist ethic of modesty and introspection, consistent with the broader religious environment of the Dutch Republic. He did not have a major patron but was supported by local collectors and the art-loving elite of Delft. Today, Vermeer's paintings are celebrated in major museums worldwide, including the Rijksmuseum, the Louvre, and the Metropolitan Museum of Art, underscoring his status as one of the foremost figures in art history for his subtle complexity and attention to the interplay of light and color.

Aegidius Sadeler (1590)

Maarten de Vos (1532-1603) was a Flemish painter based in Antwerp, noted for his significant contributions to the Northern Renaissance with his elaborate and mannerist style, characterized by its elegance and often elongated figures. De Vos was prolific across a range of subjects including altarpieces, mythological scenes, and portraits, but he particularly excelled in religious themes. His works, such as the extensive series on "The Life, Passion, and Resurrection of Christ," demonstrate his mastery in narrating complex biblical stories with rich detail and vibrant color, aimed at fostering spiritual engagement and devotion among viewers. These religious works were deeply influenced by his steadfast Catholic faith, aiming to visually translate theological themes into compelling imagery. De Vos enjoyed the patronage of Antwerp's wealthy merchant class and various religious confraternities, which enabled his artistic ventures. Today, his artworks are featured in prominent collections worldwide, including the Royal Museum of Fine Arts in Antwerp and the Prado Museum in Madrid, affirming his role as a pivotal figure in the development of Flemish art.

Self Portrait (1512-1514)

Matthias Grünewald (c. 1470-1528) was a German Renaissance painter associated with the Upper Rhine region, where he lived and worked, particularly in Mainz and Halle. He painted in the late Gothic and early Renaissance styles, known for his expressive use of color and emotive intensity. Grünewald's subjects often included religious themes, particularly scenes from the Bible and Christian iconography, characterized by their emotional depth and spiritual fervor. His religious artworks were motivated by a desire to convey the suffering and redemption central to Christian faith, exemplified in works such as the Isenheim Altarpiece, where his depiction of Christ's crucifixion reflects profound empathy and theological reflection. Grünewald's relationship with Christianity was deeply spiritual, influencing his choice of subjects and the emotional resonance of his paintings. He had patrons among religious institutions and nobility, including the monastery of St. Anthony in Isenheim, where the altarpiece remains a masterpiece of Christian art. Today, his artworks are predominantly housed in museums like the Unterlinden Museum in Colmar, France, and the Alte Pinakothek in Munich, Germany, showcasing his enduring impact on religious art during the Renaissance.

Carlo Ridolfi (1648)

Moretto da Brescia (c. 1498-1554) was an Italian Renaissance painter known for his work in Brescia, where he lived and primarily worked throughout his career. He painted in the High Renaissance style, characterized by its clarity, harmony, and attention to naturalistic detail. Moretto's subjects included religious themes, portraits, and historical scenes, often depicting saints, biblical figures, and local dignitaries with a sense of dignity and solemnity. His religious artworks were motivated by a deep piety and a desire to inspire devotion and contemplation among viewers, reflecting his strong connection to Christian faith and the teachings of the Catholic Church. Moretto had several patrons, including local nobility and religious institutions in Brescia, who commissioned works for churches and private collections. Today, much of his artwork is housed in museums and galleries across Italy, including the Pinacoteca Tosio Martinengo in Brescia and the National Gallery in London, where his religious paintings continue to be appreciated for their spiritual depth and artistic skill, showcasing his enduring legacy in Renaissance art.

DJ Kadagian is an award-winning documentary filmmaker, best-selling author, and quantum economist. His films have aired on PBS, Gaia TV, the Discovery Channel, and Hallmark, as well as being featured at over 120 film festivals around the world. In them, he has collaborated with some of the country's top philosophers, academics, activists, poets, researchers, and theologians.

His first book, *The Crossover Experience,* which explores the phenomenon of the near-death experience, was released in 2022 and has been an Amazon Best-Seller. In a followup to his bestselling *Crossover Experience*, DJ will soon be releasing *Where the Afterlife Meets Quantum Physics: Proof of the Near-Death Experience?* The book explores the remarkable similarities between the experiences reported during near-death experiences and the otherworldly realm of quantum physics. In 2023, he released *My Very Own Psychedelic Psychotherapy,* chronicling his experience with psychedelics for psycho-spiritual healing and growth. His most recent book, released in 2024, is entitled *RUMI for Kids / and the Young at Heart.* This was created in part as a natural complement to his film series *Poetry in Motion,* an innovative collection of 21 short films that artfully combines a powerful poem with music and imagery, creating a captivating experience.

Allen Dwight Callahan is a scholar and theologian recognized for his contributions to African American religious studies and biblical interpretation. Born in the United States, Callahan's academic journey has been marked by a commitment to exploring the intersection of race, religion, and social justice. He earned his Ph.D. from Harvard University and has held teaching positions at institutions such as Harvard Divinity School and the University of San Francisco.

Callahan's scholarly work focuses on the cultural and theological dimensions of African American religious traditions, particularly within the context of biblical texts and narratives. His books, including "The Talking Book: African Americans and the Bible" (2006), have been influential in reimagining the role of scripture in African American communities and beyond. Through his research, writing, and teaching, Callahan continues to inspire dialogue and critical reflection on the ways religion intersects with issues of race, identity, and liberation in contemporary society.

Richard Rohr is a Franciscan friar and prolific author whose work centers on contemplative spirituality and social justice. Ordained as a priest in 1970, Rohr integrates Franciscan wisdom with insights from psychology and theology to explore themes of transformation and the interconnectedness of all life. Through books like "The Universal Christ" (2019) and "Falling Upward" (2011), he challenges readers to embrace a deeper understanding of spirituality that transcends religious boundaries and fosters personal growth.

Founder of the Center for Action and Contemplation in New Mexico, Rohr's teachings reach a global audience through lectures, workshops, and online resources. His accessible yet profound insights have made him a leading voice in contemporary Christian thought, inspiring individuals to engage in contemplative practice and compassionate action. Richard Rohr continues to influence spiritual seekers and scholars, promoting a spirituality rooted in love, inclusivity, and a profound sense of connection to the divine and each other.

Huston Smith (1919-2016) was a renowned scholar of comparative religion and philosophy whose illustrious career spanned over six decades. Born in Suzhou, China, to Methodist missionaries, Smith's early exposure to diverse religious traditions shaped his lifelong fascination with exploring spirituality. He earned a Ph.D. in philosophy from the University of Chicago, where he later imparted his wisdom as a distinguished faculty member.

Smith's seminal work, "The World's Religions" (1958), remains a cornerstone in the study of global religious traditions, offering profound insights into their beliefs and practices. Throughout his career, he advocated for experiential understanding and respect for diverse faiths, championing religious pluralism and fostering meaningful interfaith dialogue. As a professor at Syracuse University and UC Berkeley, Smith captivated students with his engaging lectures and profound teachings. His scholarly achievements earned him prestigious accolades, including the Templeton Prize in 1996, recognizing his profound contributions to religious studies. Huston Smith's enduring legacy continues to shape global discourse on religion, promoting a deeper appreciation for spiritual diversity across cultures and generations.

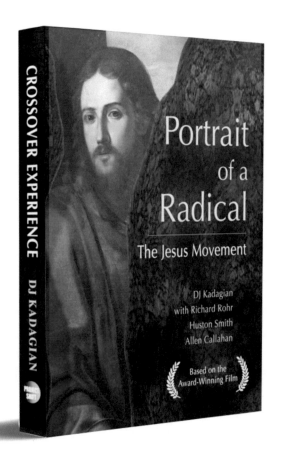

I hope you experienced as much joy reading *Portrait of a Radical* as I did in writing it. If you'd like to share your thoughts, please leave an honest review by visiting our review page using the QR code below, or on the review page of the retailer where you purchased the book. Your feedback is appreciated.

Know that reviews are an important way for readers to discover independent authors, and they provide valuable feedback that I take seriously. Each review offers insights that help me continue to refine my work and reach a broader audience. Your thoughts are appreciated and play a significant role in shaping the ongoing journey of my writing.

Thank you,

DJ Kadagian

As someone who just finished Portrait of a Radical, did you know that one of the most frequently encountered figures in near-death experiences is Jesus? In this best-selling book, discover among other things, how people describe meeting him, the vivid details of these encounters, and the profound impact they have on their lives.

In the ***Crossover Experience***, our trio of researchers delves into the finer details of NDEs. Within these often overlooked aspects, they uncover a wealth of clues that bring more depth, nuance, and meaning to what a Near-Death Experience communicates. To their surprise, they discover that it's often in what remains unseen within an NDE that we learn as much as what is.

Join us on a journey ***through 100 of the most extraordinary*** Near-Death Experiences ever recorded, in search of a deeper, more expansive understanding of what the NDE is trying to tell us. That we are far more than the physical world we perceive. We are more than our bodies. Death is not the end of our being—it is simply a transition into a broader, more profound existence.

Buy It Now!

Bibliography

Note: The entries in this bibliography are listed in the order in which they are first referenced in the book.

Introduction

Rubens, Peter Paul. Matthew the Apostle. 1612. Museo del Prado, Madrid, Spain. Faithful reproduction of a two-dimensional work of art in the public domain. Accessed June 2024. https://commons.wikimedia.org/wiki/File:Rubens_apostel_mattheus_grt.jpg

Chapter One

Kramskoy, Ivan. Christ in the Wilderness. 1872. Tretyakov Gallery, Moscow, Russia. Faithful reproduction of a two-dimensional work of art in the public domain. Accessed June 2024. https://en.wikipedia.org/wiki/File:Christ_in_the_Wilderness_-_Ivan_Kramskoy_-_Google_Cultural_Institute.jpg

Buonarroti, Michelangelo. The Torment of Saint Anthony. 1487-1488. Kimbell Art Museum, Fort Worth, Texas, USA. Faithful reproduction of a two-dimensional work of art in the public domain. Accessed June 2024. https://en.m.wikipedia.org/wiki/File:The_Torment_of_Saint_Anthony_(Michelangelo).jpg

Unknown. John the Baptist (detail from Altar Frontal from Gésera). 13th Century. Museu Nacional d'Art de Catalunya, Barcelona, Spain. Faithful reproduction of a two-dimensional work of art in the public domain. Accessed June 2024. https://www.museunacional.cat/en/colleccio/altar-frontal-gesera/anonim/035702-000

Shunmei, Ikarashi. Lau Tzu. 18th Century. The British Museum, London, United Kingdom. Faithful reproduction of a two-dimensional work of art in the public domain. Accessed June 2024. https://commons.wikimedia.org/wiki/File:Lao_Zi_by_Ikarashi_Shunmei.jpg

Reni, Guido. Moses with the Tables of the Law. 1624–25. Galleria Borghese, Rome, Italy. Faithful reproduction of a two-dimensional work of art in the public domain. Accessed June 2024. https://commons.wikimedia.org/wiki/File:Guido_Reni_-_Moses_with_the_Tables_of_the_Law_-_WGA19289.jpg

Hofmann, Heinrich. Christ in Gethsemane. 1886. Riverside Church, New York, USA. Faithful reproduction of a two-dimensional work of art in the public domain. Accessed June 2024. https://commons.wikimedia.org/wiki/File:Christ_in_Gethsemane.jpg

Unknown. Shakyamuni Buddha. 18th Century. Rubin Museum of Art, New York, USA. Faithful reproduction of a two-dimensional work of art in the public domain. Accessed June 2024. https://en.m.wikipedia.org/wiki/File:Shakyamuni_Buddha_-_Google_Art_Project.jpg

Angelico, Fra. Saint Benedict of Nursia (detail of fresco). 15th Century. Museum of San Marco, Florence, Italy. Faithful reproduction of a two-dimensional work of art in the public domain. Accessed June 2024. https://commons.wikimedia.org/wiki/File:Fra_Angelico_031.jpg

Cimabue. Saint Francis of Assisi (detail of fresco). 1278-1280. Lower Basilica of San Francesco, Assisi, Italy. Faithful reproduction of a two-dimensional work of art in the public domain. Accessed June 2024. https://commons.wikimedia.org/wiki/File:San_Francesco_Cimabue2.jpg

Angelico, Fra. Saint Dominic Adoring the Crucifixion (detail of fresco). 1442-45. Museum of San Marco, Florence, Italy. Faithful reproduction of a two-dimensional work of art in the public domain. Accessed June 2024. https://commons.wikimedia.org/wiki/File:Fra_Angelico_-Saint_Dominic_adoring_the_Crucifixion_-_San_Antonino_cloister_-_close_up_Saint_Dominic.jpeg

Rivière, Briton. The Temptation in the Wilderness. 1898. Guildhall Art Gallery & London's Roman Amphitheatre, London, United Kingdom. Faithful reproduction of a two-dimensional work of art in the public domain. Accessed June 2024. https://commons.wikimedia.org/wiki/File:Briton_Rivi%C3%A8re_-_The_Temptation_in_the_Wilderness.jpg.

Scheffer, Ary. The Temptation of Christ. 1854. Walker Art Gallery, Liverpool, United Kingdom. Faithful reproduction of a two-dimensional work of art in the public domain. Accessed June 2024. https://en.wikipedia.org/wiki/File:Ary_Scheffer_-_The_Temptation_of_Christ_%281854%29.jpg

Chapter Two

di Bondone, Giotto. The Last Judgment (detail from the Scrovegni Chapel frescoes). 1305. Scrovegni Chapel, Padua, Italy. Faithful reproduction of a two-dimensional work of art in the public domain. Accessed June 2024. https://kerdonis.fr/ZGIOTTO02/page4.html

Unknown. The Ascension of Jesus in the Guise of a Priest. 1602-1605. San Diego Museum of Art, San Diego, California, USA. Faithful reproduction of a two-dimensional work of art in the public domain. Accessed June 2024. https://commons.wikimedia.org/wiki/File:The_ascension_of_Jesus_in_the_guise_of_a_priest,_Dastan-i_Masih,_1602-05._San_Diego_Museum_of_Art.jpg

di Bondone, Giotto. Legend of St. Francis: Sermon to the Birds. 1297-1299. Basilica of San Francesco, Assisi, Italy. Faithful reproduction of a two-dimensional work of art in the public domain. Accessed June 2024. https://commons.wikimedia.org/wiki/File:Giotto_-_Legend_of_St_Francis_-_-15-_-_Sermon_to_the_Birds.jpg

da Siena, Barna. The Calling of St. Peter. 14th Century. The Collegiate Church of San Gimignano, San Gimignano, Italy. Faithful reproduction of a two-dimensional work of art in the public domain. Accessed June 2024. https://www.wikigallery.org/wiki/painting_65724/Barna-Da-Siena/The-Calling-of-St.-Peter%2C-from-a-series-of-Scenes-of-the-New-Testament

Smetham, James. Christ Preaching to the Multitudes. 1867. Private collection. Faithful reproduction of a two-dimensional work of art in the public domain. Accessed June 2024. https://commons.wikimedia.org/wiki/File:James_Smetham_-_Christ_preaching_to_the_multitudes.jpg

Hunt, William Holman. Distant View of Nazareth. 1860. Whitworth Art Gallery (University of Manchester), Manchester, UK. Faithful reproduction of a two-dimensional work of art in the public domain. Accessed June 2024. https://commons.wikimedia.org/wiki/File:William_Holman_Hunt_-_Nazareth.jpg

Sanzio, Raffaello. The Transfiguration (detail). 1516-1520. Pinacoteca Vaticana, Vatican City. Faithful reproduction of a two-dimensional work of art in the public domain. Accessed June 2024. https://commons.wikimedia.org/wiki/File:Transfiguration_Raphael.jpg

Unknown. The Life of Christ by Chinese Artist Book. 1938. Private Collection. Faithful reproduction of a two-dimensional work of art in the public domain. Accessed June 2024. https://vmfa.museum/piction/6027262-155822552/

Chapter Three

Bloch, Carl Heinrich. Sermon on the Mount. 1877. Museum of National History at Frederiksborg Castle, Hillerød, Denmark. Faithful reproduction of a two-dimensional work of art in the public domain. Accessed June 2024. https://commons.wikimedia.org/wiki/File:BSOTM.jpg

De Vos, Maarten. The Life, Passion and Resurrection of Christ Series. 1598. British Museum, London, United Kingdom. Faithful reproduction of a two-dimensional work of art in the public domain. Accessed June 2024. https://www.britishmuseum.org/collection/object/P_1930-1216-8-1

Van Gogh, Vincent Willem. The Sower. 1888. Art Institute of Chicago, Chicago, Illinois, USA. Faithful reproduction of a two-dimensional work of art in the public domain. Accessed June 2024. https://commons.wikimedia.org/wiki/File:The_Sower.jpg

Olrik, Henrik. Sermon on Mount (detail). 19th Century. Saint Matthew's Church, Copenhagen, Denmark. Faithful reproduction of a two-dimensional work of art in the public domain. Accessed June 2024. https://en.m.wikipedia.org/wiki/File:Sankt_Matthaeus_Kirke_Copenhagen_altarpiece_detail1.jpg

Tissot, James. The Tribute Money (Le denier de César). 1886-1894. Brooklyn Museum, Brooklyn, New York, USA. Faithful reproduction of a two-dimensional work of art in the public domain. Accessed June 2024. https://commons.wikimedia.org/wiki/File:Brooklyn_Museum_-_The_Tribute_Money_(Le_denier_de_C%C3%A9sar)_-_James_Tissot.jpg

Hicks, Edward. Peaceable Kingdom. 1833–1834. The Metropolitan Museum of Art, New York, New York, USA. Faithful reproduction of a two-dimensional work of art in the public domain. Accessed June 2024. https://www.metmuseum.org/art/collection/search/11081

Chapter Four

Reni, Guido. The Baptism of Christ. 1622-1623, Kunsthistorisches Museum, Vienna, Austria. Faithful reproduction of a two-dimensional work of art in the public domain. Accessed June 2024. https://commons.wikimedia.org/wiki/File:Guido_Reni_-_The_Baptism_of_Christ_-_Google_Art_Project.jpg

Nolde, Emil. Christ and the Children. 1910. Museum of Modern Art, New York, New York, USA. Faithful reproduction of a two-dimensional work of art in the public domain. Accessed June 2024. https://www.moma.org/collection/works/79494

Unknown. Christ Pantocrator Icon. 6th Century. Saint Catherine's Monastery, Mount Sinai, Egypt. Faithful reproduction of a two-dimensional work of art in the public domain. Accessed June 2024. https://commons.wikimedia.org/wiki/File:Spas_vsederzhitel_sinay.jpg

Van Gogh, Vincent Willem. The Good Samaritan. 1890. Kröller-Müller Museum, Otterlo, Netherlands. Faithful reproduction of a two-dimensional work of art in the public domain. Accessed June 2024. https://en.m.wikipedia.org/wiki/File:Van_Gogh_-_Der_barmherzige_Samariter.jpeg

Di Buoninsegna, Duccio. Christ Taking Leave of the Apostles (detail of Siena Cathedral altarpiece). 1311. Museo dell'Opera Metropolitana del Duomo, Siena, Italy. Faithful reproduction of a two-dimensional work of art in the public domain. Accessed June 2024. https://commons.wikimedia.org/wiki/File:Christ_Taking_Leave_of_the_Apostles.jpg

Van Rijn, Rembrandt. Christ and the Woman Taken in Adultery. 1644. National Gallery, London, United Kingdom. Faithful reproduction of a two-dimensional work of art in the public domain. Accessed June 2024. https://commons. wikimedia.org/wiki/File:Rembrandt_Christ_and_the_Woman_Taken_in_Adultery.jpg

Masaccio (Tommaso di Ser Giovanni di Simone). Coin in the Fish's Mouth. 1425. Basilica di Santa Maria del Carmine, Florence, Italy. Faithful reproduction of a two-dimensional work of art in the public domain. Accessed June 2024. https://commons.wikimedia.org/wiki/File:Masaccio7.jpg

Tissot, James. The Pharisees Question Jesus (Les pharisiens questionnent Jésus). 1886–1894. Brooklyn Museum, Brooklyn, New York, USA. Faithful reproduction of a two-dimensional work of art in the public domain. Accessed June 2024. https://en.wikipedia.org/wiki/File:Brooklyn_Museum_-_The_Pharisees_Question_Jesus_(Les_pharisiens_questionnent_Jésus)_-_James_Tissot.jpg

Cole, Thomas. The Pilgrim of the Cross at the End of His Journey. 1846-1848. Smithsonian Institution, Washington, D.C., USA. Faithful reproduction of a two-dimensional work of art in the public domain. Accessed June 2024. https://americanart.si.edu/artwork/pilgrim-cross-end-his-journey-study-series-cross-and-world-5078

Chapter Five

Di Bondone, Giotto. The Wedding at Cana (detail from the Scrovegni Chapel frescoes). 1305. Scrovegni Chapel, Padua, Italy. Faithful reproduction of a two-dimensional work of art in the public domain. Accessed June 2024. https://en.wikipedia.org/wiki/File:Giotto_di_Bondone_-_No._24_Scenes_from_the_Life_of_Christ_-_8._Marriage_at_Cana_-_WGA09202.jpg

De Vos, Maarten. The Wedding at Cana from The Life, Passion and Resurrection of Christ Series. 1598. British Museum, London, United Kingdom. Faithful reproduction of a two-dimensional work of art in the public domain. Accessed June 2024. https://www.britishmuseum.org/collection/object/P_1930-1216-8-1

Bloch, Carl Heinrich. Christ Healing the Sick at Bethesda. 1883. Brigham Young University Museum of Art, Provo, Utah, USA. Faithful reproduction of a two-dimensional work of art in the public domain. Accessed June 2024. https://www.churchofjesuschrist.org/media/image/pool-of-bethesda-carl-bloch-5b6576e?lang=eng

Jordaens, Jacob. St. John the Baptist. 1630. Columbus Museum of Art, Columbus, Ohio, USA. Faithful reproduction of a two-dimensional work of art in the public domain. Accessed June 2024. https://commons.wikimedia.org/wiki/File:Jacob_Jordaens_-_St._John_the_Baptist.jpg

Buonarroti, Michelangelo. Prophet Isaiah (detail, Sistine Chapel). 1512. Vatican Museums, Vatican City. Faithful reproduction of a two-dimensional work of art in the public domain. Accessed June 2024. https://commons.wikimedia.org/wiki/File:Jesaja_(Michelangelo).jpg

Chapter Six

Di Bondone, Giotto. The Wedding at Cana (detail from the Scrovegni Chapel frescoes). 1305. Scrovegni Chapel, Padua, Italy. Faithful reproduction of a two-dimensional work of art in the public domain. Accessed June 2024. https://en.wikipedia.org/wiki/File:Giotto_di_Bondone_-_No._24_Scenes_from_the_Life_of_Christ_-_8._Marriage_at_Cana_-_WGA09202.jpg

Vermeer, Johannes. Christ in the House of Martha and Mary. 1655. National Galleries Scotland, Edinburgh, Scotland. Faithful reproduction of a two-dimensional work of art in the public domain. Accessed June 2024. https://

commons.wikimedia.org/wiki/File:Johannes_(Jan)_Vermeer_-_Christ_in_the_House_of_Martha_and_Mary_-_Google_Art_Project.jpg

Rubens, Peter Paul. The Feast in the House of Simon the Pharisee. 1618-20. Hermitage Museum, Saint Petersburg, Russia. Faithful reproduction of a two-dimensional work of art in the public domain. Accessed June 2024. https://commons.wikimedia.org/wiki/File:Rubens-Feast_of_Simon_the_Pharisee.jpg

Di Bondone, Giotto. The Resurrection of Christ (detail from the Scrovegni Chapel frescoes). 1305. Scrovegni Chapel, Padua, Italy. Faithful reproduction of a two-dimensional work of art in the public domain. Accessed June 2024. https://kerdonis.fr/ZGIOTTO02/page4.html

El Greco. The Penitent Magdalene. 1576. Museum of Fine Arts, Budapest, Hungary. Faithful reproduction of a two-dimensional work of art in the public domain. Accessed June 2024. https://commons.wikimedia.org/wiki/File:El_Greco_-_The_Penitent_Magdalene_-_Google_Art_Project.jpg

Chapter Seven

Bosch, Hieronymus. HeLL. 1505. Hermitage Museum, Saint Petersburg, Russia. Faithful reproduction of a two-dimensional work of art in the public domain. Accessed June 2024. https://commons.wikimedia.org/wiki/File:Hell_(Follower_of_Bosch,_Hermitage).jpg

Di Bondone, Giotto. Scenes from the Life of Joachim (detail from the Scrovegni Chapel frescoes). 1305. Scrovegni Chapel, Padua, Italy. Faithful reproduction of a two-dimensional work of art in the public domain. Accessed June 2024. https://kerdonis.fr/ZGIOTTO02/page4.html

Buonarroti, Michelangelo. The Creation of the Sun, the Moon and the Stars (detail from the Sistine Chapel Frescoes). 1511. Sistine Chapel, Vatican City. Faithful reproduction of a two-dimensional work of art in the public domain. Accessed June 2024.https://commons.wikimedia.org/wiki/File:Michelangelo_Buonarroti_018.jpgg

Klimt, Gustav. Adam and Eve. 1917. Österreichische Galerie Belvedere, Vienna, Austria. Faithful reproduction of a two-dimensional work of art in the public domain. Accessed June 2024. https://commons.wikimedia.org/wiki/File:Michelangelo_Buonarroti_018.jpg

Poynter, Edward. The Visit of the Queen of Sheba to King Solomon. 1890. Art Gallery of New South Wales, Sydney, Australia. Faithful reproduction of a two-dimensional work of art in the public domain. Accessed June 2024. https://en.m.wikipedia.org/wiki/File:%27The_Visit_of_the_Queen_of_Sheba_to_King_Solomon%27,_oil_on_canvas_painting_by_Edward_Poynter,_1890,_Art_Gallery_of_New_South_Wales.jpg

Van Rijn, Rembrandt. Christ In The Storm On The Sea Of Galilee. 1633. Stolen from Isabella Stewart Gardner Museum, Boston, Massachusetts, USA. Faithful reproduction of a two-dimensional work of art in the public domain. Accessed June 2024. https://en.wikipedia.org/wiki/File:Rembrandt_Christ_in_the_Storm_on_the_Lake_of_Galilee.jpg

Chapter Eight

Gentileschi, Artemisia. Christ Blessing the Children. 1620-25. Museum of Modern Art, New York, New York, USA. Faithful reproduction of a two-dimensional work of art in the public domain. Accessed June 2024. https://commons.wikimedia.org/wiki/File:Sinite_Parvulos_-_A._Gentileschi.png

Honthorst, Gerard van. King David, the King of Israel. 1622. Centraal Museum, Utrecht, Netherlands. Faithful reproduction of a two-dimensional work of art in the public domain. Accessed June 2024. https://en.m.wikipedia.org/wiki/File:King_David,_the_King_of_Israel.jpg

Honthorst, Gerard van. King David, the King of Israel. 1622. Centraal Museum, Utrecht, Netherlands. Faithful reproduction of a two-dimensional work of art in the public domain. Accessed June 2024. https://en.m.wikipedia.org/wiki/File:King_David,_the_King_of_Israel.jpg

Honthorst, Gerard van. King David, the King of Israel. 1622. Centraal Museum, Utrecht, Netherlands. Faithful reproduction of a two-dimensional work of art in the public domain. Accessed June 2024. https://en.m.wikipedia.org/wiki/File:King_David,_the_King_of_Israel.jpg

Theotokopoulos, Domenikos (El Greco). Christ Cleansing the Temple. 1570. National Gallery of Art, Washington, D.C., USA. Faithful reproduction of a two-dimensional work of art in the public domain. Accessed June 2024. https://www.nga.gov/collection/art-object-page.43723.html

Di Bondone, Giotto. The Arrest of Christ (Kiss of Judas). 1305. Scrovegni Chapel, Padua, Italy. Faithful reproduction of a two-dimensional work of art in the public domain. Accessed June 2024. https://commons.wikimedia.org/wiki/File:Giotto_-_Scrovegni_-_-31-_-_Kiss_of_Judas.jpg

De Vos, Maarten. The Life, Passion and Resurrection of Christ Series. 1598. British Museum, London, United Kingdom. Faithful reproduction of a two-dimensional work of art in the public domain. Accessed June 2024. https://www.britishmuseum.org/collection/object/P_1930-1216-8-1

Chapter Nine

Orpen, Rebecca. Saint Bonaventure Inspired to Write. 1890. The National Trust, United Kingdom. Faithful reproduction of a two-dimensional work of art in the public domain. Accessed June 2024. https://commons.wikimedia.org/wiki/File:Rebecca_Dulcibella_Orpen_(1830-1923)_-_Saint_Bonaventure_Inspired_to_Write_-_343200_-_National_Trust.jpg

Doré, Gustave. Christ Leaving the Court. 1874. Strasbourg Museum of Modern and Contemporary Art, Strasbourg, France. Faithful reproduction of a two-dimensional work of art in the public domain. Accessed June 2024. https://commons.wikimedia.org/wiki/File:Le_Christ_quittant_le_pr%C3%A9toire-Gustave_Dor%C3%A9_(3).jpg

Munch, Edvard, Golgotha," 1900, Munch Museum, Oslo, Norway, Faithful reproduction of a two-dimensional work of art in the public domain, Accessed June 2024, https://commons.wikimedia.org/wiki/File:Edvard_Munch_-_Golgotha_(1900).jpg

Di Bondone, Giotto. The Lamentation of Christ (detail from the Scrovegni Chapel frescoes). 1305. Scrovegni Chapel, Padua, Italy. Faithful reproduction of a two-dimensional work of art in the public domain. Accessed June 2024. https://commons.wikimedia.org/wiki/File:Compianto_sul_Cristo_morto_(dettaglio)_(Scrovegni).jpg

Mantegna, Andrea. Crucifixion. 1457-1460. Louvre Museum, Paris, France. Faithful reproduction of a two-dimensional work of art in the public domain. Accessed June 2024. https://commons.wikimedia.org/wiki/File:Mantegna,_Andrea_-_crucifixion_-_Louvre_from_Predella_San_Zeno_Altarpiece_Verona.jpg

Rubens, Peter Paul. Christ's Apparition to the Disciples (detail from the Rockox Triptych). 1613-1615. Royal Museum of Fine Arts Antwerp, Antwerp, Belgium. Faithful reproduction of a two-dimensional work of art in the public domain. Accessed June 2024. https://commons.wikimedia.org/wiki/File:Peter_Paul_Rubens_-_Christ%27s_Apparition_to_the_Disciples_(the_Rockox_Triptych)_(cropped).jpg

Chapter Ten

Van Rijn, Rembrandt. Head of Christ. 1648. Gemäldegalerie, Berlin, Germany. Faithful reproduction of a two-dimensional work of art in the public domain. Accessed June 2024. https://commons.wikimedia.org/wiki/File: Christuskopf_-_Gem%C3%A4ldegalerie_Berlin_-_5250510.jpg

Buonarroti, Michelangelo. Creation of Adam. 1512. Sistine Chapel, Vatican City. Faithful reproduction of a two-dimensional work of art in the public domain. Accessed June 2024. https://commons.wikimedia.org/wiki/File: Michelangelo_-_Creation_of_Adam_(cropped).jpg

Bakhuizen, Ludolf. Christ in the Storm on the Sea of Galilee. 1695. Indianapolis Museum of Art, Indianapolis, Indiana, USA. Faithful reproduction of a two-dimensional work of art in the public domain. Accessed June 2024. https://commons.wikimedia.org/wiki/File:Backhuysen,_Ludolf,_I_-_Christ_in_the_Storm_on_the_Sea_of_ Galilee_-_Google_Art_Project.jpg

Signol, Émile. Taking of Jerusalem by the Crusaders. 1847. Palace of Versailles, Versailles, France. Faithful reproduction of a two-dimensional work of art in the public domain. Accessed June 2024. https://commons. wikimedia.org/wiki/File:Taking_of_Jerusalem_by_the_Crusaders,_15th_July_1099.jpg

Rubens, Peter Paul. Fall of Man. 1628-29. Mauritshuis, The Hague, Netherlands. Faithful reproduction of a two-dimensional work of art in the public domain. Accessed June 2024. https://commons.wikimedia.org/wiki/File:Jan_ Brueghel_de_Oude_en_Peter_Paul_Rubens_-_Het_aards_paradijs_met_de_zondeval_van_Adam_en_Eva.jpg

Scott, William Bell. The Rending of the Veil. 1869. Private Collection. Faithful reproduction of a two-dimensional work of art in the public domain. Accessed June 2024. https://commons.wikimedia.org/wiki/File:Rending_of_the_ veil_by_William_Bell_Scott_(1869,_priv.coll).jpg

Maes, Nicolas. Christ Blessing the Children. 1652-53. The National Gallery, London, United Kingdom. Faithful reproduction of a two-dimensional work of art in the public domain. Accessed June 2024. https://commons. wikimedia.org/wiki/File:Nicolaes_Maes_-_Christ_Blessing_the_Children_-_WGA13814.jpg

Sanzio, Raffaello. The Transfiguration. 1516-1520. Pinacoteca Vaticana, Vatican City. Faithful reproduction of a two-dimensional work of art in the public domain. Accessed June 2024. https://en.wikipedia.org/wiki/ Transfiguration_(Raphael)#/media/File:Transfiguration_Raphael.jpg

Caravaggio, Crucifixion of Saint Peter, 1600, Cerasi Chapel, Faithful reproduction of a two-dimensional work of art in the public domain, Accessed June 2024, https://commons.wikimedia.org/wiki/File:Crucifixion_of_Saint_Peter-Caravaggio_(c.1600).jpg

Catena, Vincenzo, Christ and the Samaritan Woman,1520-1530, The Columbia Museum of Art, Columbia, USA, Faithful reproduction of a two-dimensional work of art in the public domain, Accessed June 2024, https://www. columbiamuseum.org/collection-highlights/christ-and-samaritan-woman

Grünewald, Matthias, Crucifixion (Detail Isenheim Altarpiece), 1512-1516, Unterlinden Museum, Colmar, France, Faithful reproduction of a two-dimensional work of art in the public domain, Accessed June 2024, https://commons. wikimedia.org/wiki/File:Grunewald_Isenheim1.jpg

Made in the USA
Columbia, SC
19 December 2024

4f26cd47-0bec-4cb1-8c8a-9516851ad584R01